Praise for *Turkey Decoded*

'As an EU candidate country focus will be on Turkey for years to come. A future enlargement, embracing Turkey, will be a crucial and a historical step. Ann Dismorr's knowledge and deep insights about the situation in the country are invaluable.'

Carl Bildt, Swedish Foreign Minister and former Prime Minister

'Ann Dismorr's *Turkey Decoded* provides an authoritative insight into the real Turkey. For those who might still have reservations about Turkey's rightful accession into the European Union, this astute and comprehensive study should dispel all doubts.'

Moris Farhi, author of *Young Turk*

'A thoughtful and engaging book about Turkey and its relations with the European Union. It should be widely read – especially perhaps by those who try to use their recent opposition to Turkish membership of the EU to score cheap domestic political points.'

Chris Patten, former European Commissioner and Governor of Hong Kong

'A fascinating, inside account of one of Europe's largest countries.'

Margot Wallström, Vice-President, European Commission, Brussels

Ann Dismorr

TURKEY DECODED

SAQI

London San Francisco Beirut

ISBN: 978-0-86356-656-1

First published by Saqi, 2008

A full CIP record for this book is available from the British Library.
A full CIP record for this book is available from the Library of Congress.

Manufactured in Lebanon

SAQI

26 Westbourne Grove, London W2 5RH
825 Page Street, Suite 203, Berkeley, California 94710
Tabet Building, Mneimneh Street, Hamra, Beirut
www.saqibooks.com

*This book is dedicated
to the memory of Anna Lindh
and to my family
for their unwavering support*

Contents

Introduction

During my first visit to Turkey as a tourist in 1998, I stayed at a landmark hotel in the heart of historic old Istanbul, Sultanahmet, named after Sultan Ahmet I, builder of the nearby Blue Mosque. The hotel reflects the gradually changing image of Turkey. It used to be a notorious prison, located in an Ottoman building, before being transformed into a hotel. In its previous guise it resembled the setting of Oliver Stone's movie *Midnight Express* about a young American's ordeal in a Turkish prison. Remarkably, although the film is almost thirty years old, it still conveys strong images equating Turkey with prison torture. As a diplomat specializing in human rights, based in Geneva at the time, it was obvious to me that Turkey's troubled human rights record made its EU ambitions almost utopian. I never expected to be proven wrong or that I, as an ambassador from an EU country, would be part of Turkey's historic transformation, which turned out to be the case only a few years later.

A record number of tourists visited Turkey in 2005 but remarkably few among the millions of tourists realize, or want to acknowledge, that Istanbul is the largest city in Europe. Despite being part of European history for centuries, Turkey is perceived most of the time as mysteriously Oriental and distinctly different from the rest of Europe. Turkey's struggle for EU membership is in high gear despite a hardening in EU public opinion against Turkish membership and reduced support in Turkey for the EU bid. It can no longer be ignored or dismissed as a somewhat odd and persistent EU candidate country, which will remain on the fringes of Europe. A new chapter in our common history has begun. Despite the uncertainties ahead it cannot easily be reversed.

Unlike the demographic development of increasingly ageing populations in Western Europe, Turkey has Europe's fastest growing population. It will overtake Germany in about fifteen years as the most populous European country. This advance highlights its growing importance, not only politically but also from an economic and demographic viewpoint.

Today around twenty million Muslims live in European Union countries, where Islam is the fastest growing religion. In recent years, terror attacks in the US, London and Madrid have fuelled fears of radical Islam gaining support among immigrant Muslims in the West. Believers in Huntington's theory of the 'Clash of Civilizations' feel vindicated. The increasing feeling of alienation in the Muslim world towards Western policies has led to recurrent clashes of cultures. The 'cartoon crisis' after the publication in Denmark of caricatures of the Prophet Muhammad led to Muslim outrage across continents, from London to Jakarta in 2006. This was just one example of a clash between Western liberty and Muslim sensitivity, with radicals fanning the fire. Attention is turning towards Turkey's ability to bridge the deepening divide between Islam and the West.

Could Turkey, as a future EU member, provide living proof for Muslim immigrants that they are genuinely accepted by Europeans? Or will Turkey play an increasing role in domestic politics in EU countries such as Germany, France and Austria, where doubts keep growing concerning its eligibility to be a fully-fledged EU member? The growing trend of questioning Turkey's cultural credentials has been highlighted by Pope Benedict XVI, whose major vision is to reassert a Christian identity in Europe. Turkey's role as bridge or barrier between East and West will only be determined as its crucial EU future unfolds.

If Turkey's European identity is called into question, its position in the region is equally ambivalent. Turkey, a Muslim yet secular society, is emerging as a regional role model. In the aftermath of the terror attacks against the US on 11 September 2001, and during the 'war on terror', the desire to find a viable link between the Western world and Islam increased. With political support for radical Islamists spreading in various parts of the Middle East and among some Muslim immigrant communities in Western Europe, Turkey's democratization could be the only showcase for the compatibility of Islam, democracy and secularism. It is a delicate and unique balancing act that Turkey has embarked upon. The outcome will have consequences reaching far beyond its borders.

The democratization of Turkey is being closely followed in the Middle East. Arab media give extensive coverage of the Turkish EU application process. Turkey has embarked on a new and assertive foreign policy. It is reaching out to its Arab neighbours in a proactive and unprecedented way, while enjoying uniquely excellent relations with Israel. However, ambivalent sentiments against Turkey linger in Arab states. The memory of Turkey's colonial past during the Ottoman Empire is surprisingly alive almost a hundred years later. I experienced it first-hand during my traditional farewell visits to the leaders in Lebanon, with whom I met as I was preparing to leave Beirut and move to my next posting as an ambassador in Ankara.

The US, like the United Kingdom, has always been an active and vocal supporter of Turkey's EU ambitions. Turkish democratization fitted in well with the central aim of the Bush administration's foreign policy: to promote democracy in the Middle East. However, the war in Iraq has severely dented the traditionally close ties between Ankara and Washington. Turkey's sensational refusal to facilitate the US-led invasion in 2003 shook the foundations of the relationship of the two NATO allies. The rift that occurred as a result, together with disparate views on how to deal with Kurdish issues in northern Iraq, have undermined their previously cordial relationship. With no end in sight to the Iraqi war, the potential for further serious setbacks in US–Turkish relations are plentiful.

When I moved to Ankara in 2001 as the Swedish ambassador, with my young daughter in tow, the prospect of Turkey becoming a European Union member still appeared distant, if not unlikely. Turkey had by then been waiting for a breakthrough in its EU process for almost forty years. Officially there was no questioning of Turkey's eligibility for membership over these years. On the contrary, it was confirmed on many occasions, but accompanied by consistent messages from the European Union that the political and economic conditions had to improve substantially before accession talks could begin. Few expected Turkey to be able to transform itself sufficiently, including the Turks themselves.

Wherever I went, whether in shops or at official functions, I was met with the question: 'Why does the EU not accept Turkey?' It was posed by people of all ages and backgrounds. The question reflected the passionate pursuit of a long-held dream of Turkish EU membership. It also reflected a sense of being misunderstood and discriminated against. The depth of emotions about EU–Turkish relations came initially as a surprise to me as a Western European, where EU membership rarely evokes strong and widespread feelings.

It was around Christmas time in the Finnish capital of Helsinki when the distant prospect of Turkey joining the expanding European Union turned into a genuine possibility. The year was 1999. Only after lengthy and heated negotiations was an agreement reached to grant Turkey candidate status. The fundamental question of whether a poor, populous and Muslim country belonged in the Western European bloc was not raised but was put on the back burner in the aftermath of the Helsinki negotiations.

Paradoxically, it took a pro-Islamic conservative government to achieve far-reaching democratic reforms in Turkey, transforming the country. A silent revolution of human rights reforms was spearheaded by the young and charismatic Recep Tayyip Erdoğan, a former convicted Islamist, and his newly founded Justice and Development (AK) Party. As Erdoğan's political star started to ascend in the run-up to the elections in 2002, so did the personal criticism against him in various circles. His allegedly expensive tastes and Italian tailor-made suits received media attention. For a politician with his roots and appeal among the underprivileged it was an image that could be counter-productive. These issues were in contrast to my first encounter with Tayyip Erdoğan at the airport in Ankara well before the election: his stature and charisma were striking, but his clothes unnoticeable.

Erdoğan's AK Party swept into power in 2002 after an unexpected landslide election victory. There was deep-rooted scepticism and mistrust among the Turkish establishment against the newly elected government. The staunchly secular establishment feared there was a hidden, religious agenda. Those sentiments were shared by many within the EU.

Will Turkey's Prime Minister Erdoğan be the last Islamist or the first democrat? He has to choose between the two alternatives. That was the argument in a domestic debate before the Turkish leader joined a G8 meeting in the summer of 2004 when the US strategy of fostering democracy in the Middle East took centre stage. It coincided with a time when Turkey was on the brink of a historic breakthrough in its relations with the European Union.

After intense effort the AK Party government obtained a green light for EU membership talks at an historic summit in Brussels in December 2004. It succeeded where its predecessors had failed for decades.

Shortly after my move to Ankara a political storm erupted regarding a Swedish publication. It contained some controversial opinions on Turkish identity as well as on the Armenian massacres at the beginning of the twentieth century. The controversy resulted in a violent response from ultra-nationalists, who sent me daily death threats for months. Nothing had prepared me for the emotions of aggressive nationalism in Turkey. I quickly learnt that taboos were still very much a reality.

Step by step the taboos, existing since the founding days of the Turkish Republic in the 1920s, were broken. The attempt to negotiate entry into the European Union led to increased freedom and tolerance. The Kurdish issue was no longer a forbidden topic. A cautious process of reconciliation between the state and the Kurds has so far not been derailed despite renewed violence by fringe groups of Kurdish terrorists. Calls for further reforms and freedoms for the Kurds are on the increase. Without the prospect of EU membership the future of the impoverished Turkish Kurdish-populated southeast is uncertain. The developments in war-torn Iraq and the flourishing existence of Kurds in northern Iraq have resulted in a new assertiveness among Kurds. These factors add to the complexity of the Kurdish issue in Turkey. They could once again become a stumbling-block on Turkey's road towards EU membership, just as they did in the 1990s.

During extensive travels in southeastern Turkey, I met with many women's organizations, all recalling different stories of discrimination and violence. Sometimes the violence turned deadly, especially with 'honour' crimes within the family against young girls and women. Strikingly, many women attach high hopes for a better future to Turkey becoming an EU member. Talking to these committed women was touching and inspirational but it also felt like moving back in time, sometimes centuries. Existence for women in Turkey varies hugely. Some of the top business leaders and many academics are women, yet as many as seven million females are illiterate. Women in Turkey live with an unusual mixture of traditions and transformations. Being one of only four female ambassadors in a diplomatic corps of more than ninety countries represented, I lived and worked in a predominantly male and Muslim society. My gender opened doors through which only women could enter. My English husband, on the other hand, as the spouse of an ambassador, entered into a territory traditionally only occupied by women.

The Turkish government's ability to sustain and implement the various reforms, ranging from women's rights to increased freedom of expression, will be a litmus test for the ruling Justice and Development (AK) Party. The AK Party is searching for ways to combine the increasing demands of its large groups of religious supporters, who want more freedom and tolerance, with a traditionally staunchly secular society. Suspicion of the AK Party government's attempt to move Turkey from secularism to Islamism is still very much alive, especially among the old establishment. The AK Party's resounding victory in the 2007 parliamentary and presidential elections only fuelled these anxieties. The controversial ban in Turkey on Muslim headscarves at schools, universities and other state institutions is one of the most infected political issues. It is still unresolved and is polarizing Turkish society. During my four years in Turkey I was often approached by frustrated women wearing headscarves. They felt misunderstood by the West and marginalized by their own society. Most of the leaders of the AK Party government, including Prime Minister Erdoğan, have wives and daughters who wear headscarves. Pressure is growing at grass-roots level to ease these restrictions, something which is vehemently opposed by the staunchly secular forces. They are fearful of Turkey going down the same road as Iran. As a result there is a growing and dangerous rift between these different circles.

Tayyip Erdoğan's single-mindedness and passion to bring Turkey to the EU negotiation table in Brussels came across clearly at my first meeting with him in 2002 at the AK Party headquarters shortly after the election victory. His commitment was infectious in its clarity. Rumours that he, as a deeply pious man, would not shake hands with me, a woman, and that he would interrupt our meeting when the nearby mosque called for prayer time at sunset turned out to be completely wrong.

Despite a slowdown of the reform process since 2005, the buzz of change is penetrating Turkey. A social transformation is taking place. The democratization process took off with unprecedented commitment and speed at the beginning of the new millennium. Turkey now needs to show that the silent revolution of reforms is not a contemporary milestone which in the end turns out to be nothing but a historical footnote.

Enlargement has been the biggest success story of the EU in recent times, but its future is far from guaranteed. The EU expansion could already have reached its high-water mark. The backlash against enlargement, growing Euro-scepticism and the deepening divide between Islam and the West fuel fear of EU rejection of Turkey at the end of the process. Renewed violence in the Kurdish southeast creates anxiety of a return to the 'bad old days' of coups and undemocratic regimes. Equally, a scenario with a disillusioned Turkey turning its back to the EU cannot be excluded. What would the alternatives and consequences be?

A closer alliance for Turkey with the US and Israel is one option. Another is an alliance with its former arch-enemy Russia and the Turkic republics, which is sometimes viewed as an alternative to the 'Christian Club' of the EU. Closer ties to Middle Eastern Sunni-dominated states like Saudi Arabia and Egypt is another possible route. The reform process in Turkey could run out of steam while domestic forces opposing human rights and democratization are gaining ground. An upsurge of Turkish ultra-nationalism might happen, which was the case during the pre-election period in 2007, especially if the EU appears to have double standards towards its longest waiting applicant country. A continued deadlock on the Cyprus issue could fuel those sentiments. A return to a more assertive role for the military is likely if there is domestic political instability. The bitter presidential contest in Turkey in 2007 illustrated the readiness of the military to re-enter the political stage during turbulent times. Turkey could be tempted to become politically inward-looking and self-contained, as it was during the long period following the death of Turkey's founding father and leader Atatürk in 1938. The European Union would then lose a partner with increasing clout and credentials in international affairs.

Atatürk pointed towards Europe as the future for his country more than seventy-five years ago. His staunchly secular state is now being transformed by the AK Party and its leader Erdoğan, a conservative, devout Muslim, who is often described as the main reformist since Atatürk. My personal insights into the new political leadership and its policy are an account of a historical period when the AK Party transformed and brought Turkey into a new era in its relations with Europe. The political opposition is deeply divided, which contributed to the huge election success of the AK Party in the summer of 2007. This party is likely to remain a major political player, whether or not it will remain in power beyond the next election, scheduled for 2011. Surprisingly little has been written about this political party, which seems to be the one that will shape Turkey's future for years to come. Attention has mainly focused on the different personalities and Islamic past of Tayyip Erdoğan and Abdullah Gül.

Turkey does not fit into any easy category. It is perhaps best described as a kaleidoscope with several shifting images. Learning more and trying to understand Turkey will be essential to comprehending future developments. Turkey will remain in the headlines on a wide range of topics: European and Middle Eastern politics; the Kurdish and other human rights issues; changing US–Turkish relations; terrorism; bridging the divide between the West and Islam; demographics; and its potential as the next economic miracle.

The quest to join Europe might come full circle around the year 2014, when EU–Turkish accession talks are expected to finish. The moment of truth will then arrive. Fully-fledged EU membership is far from certain. Both the EU and Turkey must decide where Turkey belongs, what the future holds for them, and what directions to take. Either way, the decision will have far-reaching and long-lasting consequences for Europe as a whole.

ONE

Turkish Identity

The causes of the decline of the Ottoman Empire bore until recently striking parallels with modern Turkey: a struggle between conservative pro-Islamic forces and Western reforms; conflicts between ethnic groups; interfering foreign powers; hostile neighbours; and poor financial management. The ongoing transformation is moving Turkey away from many of these parallels and comparisons. The self-doubt and agonizing of the past now seem increasingly rare and irrelevant. Turkey is starting to look into its future in a new and more assertive way. A renewal of Turks' self-confidence is budding.

This attitude is different from the one I first encountered in 2001. Sitting by a pool in the south of France, a close English friend of mine was briefing me on Turkey before my departure. He was an expert after years of being responsible for Turkey in a world-leading financial institution. 'You must never give straightforward advice: turn it into a question instead. Turks have low self-confidence and loathe being told what should be done.' I did not quite believe it until shortly afterwards, when I received an almost identical message from a top official at the Foreign Ministry in Ankara during a courtesy call.

At the time when I learnt of my posting to Turkey as the new Swedish ambassador, I was enjoying life in Lebanon, living in the eastern, Muslim part of central Beirut with my ten-year-old daughter. When I told her we were moving to Turkey in two months' time, she dashed out of the room. Thinking it was fear of the sudden move to a completely unknown country, I expected to find her in tears. Instead, I found that she had run to her computer, looked up Turkey and had its national anthem playing loudly while she checked out the country in which she would spend her next four years. Her initial positive attitude was a wonderful relief and a great start to our new life in Turkey.

Arriving in the capital, Ankara, on a sunny August day in 2001, what first struck me was all the greenery. Ankara is often described as a dull and grey city. I was pleasantly surprised. There were even birches, the most Scandinavian of all trees, around the Parliament. Most striking were the people. Their sheer numbers and their homogeneous appearance were most noticeable as we were driving along the main boulevard upon arrival. Centuries of influxes of people from the Balkans and the Caucasus are obviously a reality but not immediately noticeable.

There were remarkably few foreigners. The foreign community in Ankara, a city of four million people, was tiny. Diplomats with their families and staff at international organizations were almost the only ones. The expatriate business community was almost exclusively living in Istanbul, the commercial hub of Turkey. Apart from my years living in Riyadh in Saudi Arabia, long before the foreign embassies moved there from Jeddah, I had never lived in a capital so unknown to most foreigners and with such an astonishingly small foreign community. Ankara felt like an adventure from day one.

Early Turkish modernization: From fez to hat

The founder and leader of the Turkish Republic, Mustafa Kemal, caused shock waves when he wore a Western-style Panama hat for the first time in the summer of 1925.[1] The reaction was all the more poignant since it took place during a visit to the conservative province of Kastamonu in the Islamic heartland of the country. Appearing in a white European summer suit and a hat, he was dressed as an infidel in the eyes of the villagers he visited. Through this bold and strongly symbolic gesture he relegated the fez, a form of Muslim headgear, to the past. It was part of the revolutionary modernization that Mustafa Kemal launched against conservative and deeply religious forces. Clothing took on a symbolic and secular meaning.

The replacement of the fez, an old symbol of Islamic orthodoxy and the Ottoman era, in favour of a European style was turned into new legislation. A Hat Law was passed by the National Assembly in November 1925, actually forbidding men to wear the fez and making hats obligatory. Reactions were mixed. European-style headgear was swiftly adopted among politicians, professionals and others belonging to the upper and middle classes, while many others reacted with resentment and in some instances with violence. In the rural eastern parts of Turkey, the Hat Law resulted in riots and mass demonstrations, many under green, Islamic flags.

Mustafa Kemal's plan to create a secular and modern state where clothing had a powerful role had made important headway. It did not happen without some ruthless methods being used to enforce the new law. While these reforms were introduced for men, the tradition of women wearing a veil was left uncontested at the time. It was regarded as too delicate a challenge to take on.

The Muslim world outside Turkey at the time showed no obvious signs of disapproval of the new dress code. An official Turkish delegate, dressed in Western attire, attended an Islamic meeting in Mecca in the 1920s and was politely received by his foreign colleagues, who were all wearing traditional robes and turbans.[2]

---

1. Patrick Kinross, *Atatürk: The rebirth of a nation*, Phoenix, 1995, p. 412.
2. P. Kinross, *Atatürk*, p. 416.

Modernization and Muslim headscarves

More than eighty years after the controversial ban on the fez, Turkey is still struggling with the symbolism of its dress code. The contested Muslim headscarves on women, a common sight on streets across the country today, have taken on a similar charged symbolism. A ban was introduced as recently as 1997, soon after the ousting of the Islamic government. Turkey's first ruling Islamic party was removed from power when the military intervened once again. The country returned to its secular course. Headscarves were from then on no longer allowed in public institutions and universities.

The headscarf represents a serious threat to the staunchly secular state, according to *Kemalists*, who are the ideological heirs of Kemal Atatürk. This almost century-old ideology (from 1919) has no strict definition, leaving it open to different interpretations. As time has passed, the basic principle has been to try to follow whatever Atatürk would have wanted. The core values are those of Turkish nationalism and secularism.

Those values are ardently guarded by the secular establishment. This body is traditionally made up of the military, the president of the country, the judiciary, bureaucracy and intelligentsia. The Republican People's party (CHP), founded by Atatürk, is the standard-bearer of Kemalism among the political parties. Kemalism permeates the country, although currently to a lesser extent under the pro-Islamic government, some would argue. Turkey might gradually be moving into a new, post-Kemalist era.

Guardians of Atatürk's stringent secularism regard the ban on Muslim headscarves in public institutions as simply non-negotiable. To lift the ban would be unconstitutional. References are made to the Constitution, the longest and most detailed that Turkey has ever had, which was adopted during the military regime in 1983. To many secular Turks the headscarf represents backwardness and is seen as a setback to the modernization of the country. To others, it is viewed as a matter of individual choice and freedom of religion.

Turkey has so far managed to be unique in balancing religion with secularism. Tolerance towards different lifestyles has long been part of the Turkish image. A girl dressed in a miniskirt next to a fully-covered woman is not an unusual sight in major cities such as Istanbul, Ankara or Izmir.

A fashion show was hosted in Istanbul by Prime Minister Erdoğan's wife during an international conference on women's rights in early 2006, in which I participated. The setting was a historical ruin, newly renovated, on the edge of the Bosporus. Models were strolling down the catwalk in front of Emine Erdoğan and her stunning daughters, who were covered in headscarves and traditional cloaks from shoulder to ankle. The contrast with the scarcely-dressed Turkish models in front of the Erdoğan family was stark. Everyone enjoyed the show. Such is the Turkey of today.

Often women, as well as some men, that I met expressed their belief that the headscarf issue is now a matter for the EU. This was particularly the case after Turkey was set to start membership negotiations. The opinion was held regardless of whether people were for or against the ban. It showed an inadequate awareness of the pluralism that exists within EU countries, where different rules apply, for example, to allowing religious symbols in schools. France and Britain apply opposite policies, with France bringing in a recent ban on religious symbols, like headscarves, in public schools. It also illustrated an unrealistic expectation of having the issue referred to Brussels to solve. But the reaction is understandable, since it has the potential to seriously polarize society.

The wife of the current president, Mrs Gül, who wears a headscarf, brought a legal case against Turkey to the European Court of Human Rights. She was unable to return to higher education after having raised her children, due to the ban on headscarves at Turkish universities. Hayrünnisa Gül chose to drop the case at the Strasbourg-based court in early 2003 when her husband became prime minister in the first AK Party government. It was viewed as detrimental to pursue legal proceedings against your own husband's government.

I met with Hayrünnisa Gül on several occasions, including at a few tea parties for ambassadors' spouses that she hosted. That I was included illustrates how I, as a female ambassador, was often lucky enough to belong in two worlds. Mrs Gül always wore her headscarf inside her house, although there were only female guests present. I could not resist comparing this to similar situations I had witnessed in Lebanon. Muslim women that I met there, who wore headscarves, usually took them off in private when no men were present.

One explanation could be that the tea parties were fairly formal, despite the wonderfully relaxed and friendly atmosphere that Mrs Gül always created in the official residence of the foreign minister, where she lived with her young family until they moved a block away into the presidential palace in 2007. I still have a small, pretty brooch, shaped as a rose, as a fond memory of one of those afternoons. Gül means 'rose' in Turkish.

Atatürk's impact and Westernization

On every 10 November, the anniversary of Atatürk's death, air raid sirens mark the exact time of his passing. At 9.05 in the morning, the intense traffic noise outside my embassy calmed down. Many stopped their cars and spent a minute's silence to honour the founding father. His picture was in the corner of every TV channel throughout the day, including MTV.

His myth and memory are sacred to many Turks. The cult surrounding his legacy is unique for a democratic country. It is difficult to comprehend without having lived in Turkey. It became a concrete reality as I was searching for postcards during my first week in the country. The newspaper shop at the Sheraton Hotel sold plenty of postcards but there was only one choice; different pictures of Atatürk. It is remarkable that a leader who founded and radically transformed Turkey is relatively unknown outside his own country.

Atatürk, himself an Ottoman Muslim from the Balkans (Macedonia), initiated revolutionary changes to move his country towards the West. The objective was 'to become a civilized nation', in Atatürk's own, plain-speaking words. Today, there is a general preference towards labelling it modernization rather than Westernization.

Atatürk's legacy has been guarded over the decades by the establishment with the military as its backbone. To a Westerner it is difficult to comprehend the depth of respect the military enjoys. It is generally regarded as competent, classless and incorrupt. Only in recent years have Prime Minister Erdoğan and his party been able to compete in surveys for the position of most trusted institution in the country. For years it was always the military or the then President Sezer, with his non-political background but seeing himself as a guardian of secularism, who came out on top.

I came across a surprisingly large number of people who still view the military as a safety net or a protector, who would step in and rescue the country when democracy appeared threatened. Despite the reduced political role of the military that perception still persists. These sentiments will increase if the rift keeps growing between secular and anti-secular forces. During the political stand-off in spring 2007 between the secular establishment and the AK government, the military assumed the lead on behalf of the secularists.

Despite EU reforms resulting in a less powerful military, the armed forces have still significant political influence. Military members of the powerful National Security Council (NSC), a body of Turkey's political and military leaders, continue to give their views on domestic and foreign policy. Opinions are expressed on issues such as terrorism, Iraq, Cyprus, secularism and EU–Turkish relations. The top military commanders are easy to spot at receptions and other official functions. They are always surrounded by huge crowds of journalists. One of them, a political commentator, once reflected to me that 'We journalists treat the military like pop stars. We also have a responsibility, as part of the EU reform process, not to hang onto their every word'.

Mistrust of foreigners

The transformation from an empire to a nation state left deep scars. Mistrust of foreigners and fear of Turkey being carved up between different powers runs deep. The Allies' peace terms for the Ottoman Empire, in the 1920 Sèvres Treaty, aimed to split Anatolia between British, French, Greek and Italian regions. In the east, there were plans for an autonomous Kurdistan and an independent Armenia. The Straits would be under international control.

The treaty was never ratified. The Ottoman Empire was not dismembered. History under Atatürk took another turn. In 1923, the Lausanne Treaty provided independence and international legitimacy for the new Turkey. Anatolia remained within its borders. Apprehension, though, of the Sèvres syndrome, is still alive in the minds of some Turks. The EU membership process is sometimes accused of being nothing but a modern version of the Sèvres Treaty. The anxiety that Turkey risks being divided in the future is particularly alive in the Kurdish regions in the east.

'The Turk's only friend is another Turk' is often quoted by Turks to illustrate how deep mistrust towards foreigners runs. It was frequently brought up when the EU was regarded as having pushed for too much too soon. This was particularly the case when Kurdish rights were promoted by the EU, which was accused of (however unwillingly) playing into the hands of ultra-nationalists.

The US-led war in Iraq, launched in 2003, has also created deep apprehension in Turkey. There is fear of threats against its territorial integrity, especially on its eastern border with Iraq. In the eventuality of an independent Kurdistan emerging in northern Iraq, Turks fear a dangerous spillover effect on its own Kurdish southeastern areas. Frequent cross-border attacks into Turkey by the Kurdistan Workers' Party, PKK, with bases in northern Iraq, led to significant Turkish military strikes in the Qandil mountains inside Iraq in late 2007, adding strain to an already complex situation. The Iraq War has also fuelled strong anti-American sentiment across the country.

As in most other countries, xenophobia exists in Turkey. It often expresses itself in an aggressively defensive approach towards Westerners. The very few times I came across it, it was based on the assumption that the West patronized Turkey and did not view or treat it as an equal. Apart from xenophobia based on nationalism there was also the factor of race. Sometimes there was a mixture of both.

Adolf Hitler's *Mein Kampf* became a surprising best-seller in Turkey in early 2005. This sudden and alarming interest in the book was rarely debated or analyzed. The small Jewish community, a total of around 30,000 in the whole country, kept a low profile. At the time, the idea that Turkey was being treated unfairly by the EU was being promoted by the ultra-nationalists. So was the theory, existing in some circles, of a Jewish–US conspiracy in the region. Hitler's book was recommended reading by the ultra-nationalist party, the MHP, and was sold at a remarkably low price. The hardworking US ambassador in Turkey at the time, Eric Edelman, had to live with frequent anti-American confrontations, which were sometimes mixed with anti-Semitism. Supportive remarks from Foreign Minister Gül did not soften some of the personal attacks against the US envoy, but his support was still an important gesture.

A strongly anti-American book, *Metallic Storm*, appeared at around the same time. The book, written by two completely unknown, young authors, soared to the top of the best-selling lists. It was the talk of the town and 'everyone' seemed absorbed by it, including the Foreign Ministry in Ankara. Rumours were ripe that the writers, surprisingly well versed in security matters, had received extensive background briefing from the military. The novel concludes with the then Foreign Minister Gül being arrested by Americans while visiting New York.

The fact that the US government initially stopped the Turkish army from entering into northern Iraq to pursue the Kurdish terrorist organization, the PKK, made a deep impression on Turkish perceptions. The US now appears to be tolerating Turkish ground and air incursions into the Kurdish parts of Iraq. Before this there was a sense of déjà vu. Turkey yet again felt alone and misunderstood in its struggle against Kurdish terrorism. When a team of Turkish Special Forces on a mission in Iraq was arrested, blindfolded and hooded by US soldiers, shock waves coursed through Turkey. The insult and defamation are still lingering in the Turkish psyche, long after the incident took place in the summer of 2004. A movie entitled *Valley of the Wolves – Iraq* in 2006 portrayed an imaginary revenge against Americans.

The so-called Turks

When existing dogmas are questioned the debate usually gets emotional. Allegations turn harsh and uncompromising. The Turkish columnist Elif Şafak highlighted the new usage of the expression 'so-called Turks'. It was increasingly used against those criticizing 'this exquisite republic founded by Atatürk'. One is then branded a traitor, wrote Şafak in the *Turkish Daily News*.[1] 'If a foreigner eavesdropped on this discourse, they would think that we Turks are divided among ourselves into three groups; the so-called Turks (the minority), the beloved Turks (the majority) and the 100 per cent Turks (the guardians of hegemony).'

Debates on taboos, for example on what happened to Armenians in Turkey at the end of World War I, have ended too frequently in hateful accusations. Tolerance levels are still remarkably restricted on a few specific issues although things are slowly changing for the better. But the murder of the Turkish-Armenian journalist Hrant Dink in early 2007 was a bitter setback for a more tolerant Turkey. Mr Dink was facing several criminal charges for his non-violent views on some

1.   4 December 2005.

highly controversial historical events. His funeral turned into a mass demonstration of solidarity but fear exists that full justice will never be served against the perpetrators. Those who dare to challenge existing beliefs are sometimes faced with trials and anonymous death threats. Turkey's most internationally well-known novelist and Nobel laureate Orhan Pamuk is one example. His remarks in a Swiss newspaper on the massacres of Armenians and Kurds almost one hundred years ago resulted in tremendously strong reactions in nationalistic circles. Legal proceedings were initiated against him despite EU protests.

Despite many setbacks and authoritarian traditions, the 'coming-out process' in Turkey has taken off. A more open and tolerant society is gradually emerging, where diverging views on taboo subjects are starting to be expressed. It would be difficult to turn back the clock. Turkey is learning to speak up.

Language and geography

Who is a Turk? With challenges and perceived threats from the outside world, real or not, the question has resurfaced in public debate in Turkey. It is also increasingly often asked by those EU countries sceptical of admitting Turkey as a full member.

When language and geography are used against Turkey becoming an EU member, the arguments are flawed. 'Turkish is not an Indo-European language,' emphasized one of the most vocal opponents of a Turkish EU membership, former French president Valéry Giscard d'Estaing. This argument has been overtaken by events. Finland has been an EU member since 1995 and Finnish is not an Indo-European language but is closely related to Turkish. So are Hungarian and Estonian, two more recent additions to the list of official EU languages.

Within Turkey, a number of different languages and dialects are spoken by Turkish citizens in their daily lives. Among these are Kurdish, Arabic and Lazz, while Turkish is the only official language.

That the European part of Turkey only compromises 3 per cent of the total land area is another argument used against Turkey's EU bid. This fails to take into account that Ankara is geographically located to the west of Cyprus, which in turn is geographically further south than Tunisia.

Religion

Turkey is alone in the Islamic world in its strict separation of religion and state. The secular order and the role of religion in society are outlined in articles 14 and 24 of the Turkish Constitution from the early 1980s. These articles are often quoted in public debates. The US Constitution is probably the only other constitution in the world that enjoys such familiarity among its citizens.

In a democracy whose population is 99 per cent Muslim, religion is banned from official life. But religious identity is still written on every Turkish ID card. Non-Muslim religious minorities, who are still facing difficulties, are thus unnecessarily exposed. The EU has so far failed in its attempts to have the Turkish authorities delete it from the cards. To find a more permissive way for religion in national life will be Turkey's toughest challenge apart from obtaining membership to the EU. The main controversies are seldom on substantive religious issues but on symbolism. In this, the headscarf is by far the most emotionally charged.

The government's appointment of key positions, such as the head of the Central Bank, created a major controversy. The Central Bank is one of Turkey's genuinely independent institutions. A battle of wills followed in spring 2006 between the government, the president and the business elite when the first choice of the Erdoğan government was an executive at an Islamic-style bank. Another potential candidate had a wife who wore a headscarf, which resulted in a raging debate. The appointment of the government's would-be candidate was vetoed by the then President Sezer, who never hesitated to take a stand against what he viewed as the government's religious tendencies. The growing gap between the rulers and the secular business elite contributed to a month-long stand-off. A political crisis was inevitable. The appointment was later withdrawn and Durmuş Yilmaz, an experienced and widely respected banker, was named Central Bank Governor in April 2006. The crisis exposed a growing unease between the ruling party and the business establishment.

The politically motivated murder in Ankara of a top judge, who had ruled against headscarves, renewed the tensions in May 2006 between the old, secular establishment and the AK Party Government. There are no statistics showing how many Turkish women wear headscarves but it is frequently cited at around 60 per cent of the female population. The numbers vary greatly across the country. Remote and rural areas show almost exclusive use of headscarves among girls, from the age of puberty, and women.

The overwhelming majority of Turks are Sunni Muslims. But the EU process has put the spotlight on religious diversity within the Turkish Muslim population. The largest is the religious and cultural group of the Alevis, who make up around one fifth of the Turkish population.[1] They are Shi'i Muslims who, unlike the Sunni Muslims, claim that Prophet Muhammad's son-in-law, Ali, and his descendants are the only rightful rulers of the community. The Alevis in Turkey are increasingly vocal in their demands. This includes claiming their own places of worship, called *Cem* houses. Unlike in mosques, men and women pray together, facing each other.

The Alevis are not officially recognized as a religious community. One senior civil servant told me over a cup of coffee that he, an Alevi, had kept his religion a secret throughout his long career. He did it to avoid discrimination but as he was retiring he no longer needed to hide it. It was explained without any obvious bitterness, just as something that had to be accepted.

Alevis do not observe some of the pillars of Islam, such as the pilgrimage to Mecca, daily prayers and fasting. When I first arrived I was informed that there would be no problem arranging lunch

1.   Ipak Ruzkan, Common Ground News Service, 10 March 2006.

meetings during Islam's month of fasting. The Turkish word for the ninth, holy month of the Islamic lunar calendar is *Ramazan*, while it is *Ramadan* in the rest of the Muslim world. Few Turks observe the strict dawn-to-dusk fasting, I was told. Most civil servants, among them Turkish diplomats, would be unlikely to follow this religious requirement. Well, after hosting several luncheons when every single Turkish guest declined, although without giving fasting as a reason, I stopped. It did not feel quite right either. *Ramazan* has some similarities with Lent, as both Muslims and Christians aim to rise above the flesh and gain more spiritual awareness.

While travelling outside Ankara during *Ramazan* I found the same pattern existed. Almost everyone I met abstained from food, drink and cigarettes from dawn to dusk. That included governors, the powerful state representatives in the regions, local politicians and people working for non-governmental organizations. Towards the end of the day the lack of liquid, especially in the heat, led to cracked lips and exceptionally dry mouths among those fasting. It was very apparent as they spoke. As a non-Muslim I was always offered something to drink but I preferred to take it out of sight and always recommended visitors to do the same.

A drummer walked by our residence in the heart of Ankara at around three o'clock every single morning during *Ramazan*. Although our residence was surrounded by a large and lush embassy garden with century-old trees, he could be heard a long way away in our bedrooms. His duty was to awaken the faithful so that they could eat before sunrise. On the last morning of *Ramazan* he went around collecting rewards from the neighbourhood. The drumming was a custom I had never come across before while living in Riyadh and Beirut. A Muslim friend of mine suggested it was probably not needed there. 'They never go to sleep during *Ramadan* and therefore do not need a drummer to wake them up,' he jested.

Turkey's religious revival has been compared to that in Britain after the industrial revolution. According to the acclaimed British author and authority on Turkey, Andrew Mango, piety is easing the pain and discomfort of Turkey's modernization. It is 'not a sign of a coming clash of civilizations, but a common feature in the development of our universal civilization,' argues Mango in his book *The Turks of Today*.[1]

Ethnicity

The fault line between Sunnis and Alevis is mostly unknown outside the borders of Turkey. That is in contrast to the dividing line between secularists and Islamic traditionalists, which is closely followed in the Muslim world, within the EU and beyond.

The dividing line between Turks and Kurdish nationalists is another internationally well-known division in Turkish society. More than fifteen years of bloody warfare between the army and the separatist Kurdish Workers' Party (PKK) left more than 30,000 dead. The renewed violence, started by the PKK in 2005, is opening up old wounds. It makes peace, reconciliation and enhanced cultural rights for the Kurds more important than ever. At the same time the violence renders that more difficult to achieve. A precarious 'Catch 22' situation has been created.

A uniting identity

The rift between Turks and Kurdish nationalists or separatists often overshadows the fact that a large majority feel a strong pride in being Turkish, united by history, culture and language. Among Turkish diplomats frequent proud references to its rich history occur in a way I have seldom come across from other European colleagues. The exhibition 'Turks, a journey of a thousand years, 600–1600', shown at the Royal Academy of Arts in London during spring 2005 reflected this pride and a new assertion of Turkey's rich heritage. The exhibition gave a spectacular illustration of the Turkic people's long journey through Central Asia, the Middle East and Europe.

1. Andrew Mango, *The Turks of Today*, John Murray, 2004, p. 11.

Overwhelming joy and patriotism swept across Turkey after the unexpected success in the Football World Cup in June 2003. Celebrations after the Turkish team won third prize went on in the streets of Ankara well after midnight with cars hooting and people singing, as though after wedding celebrations.

Turkey's Sertab Erener won the Eurovision Song Contest in 2003 with the catchy tune 'Every Way That I Can', a mix of Western and Oriental melodies. While many Europeans dismiss the contest as kitsch and irrelevant, I often heard Turks commenting after the victory that 'this really proves that we are Europeans'.

When all EU ambassadors were invited the following year to the song contest, hosted by Istanbul in May 2004, the rotating EU president (Ireland) asked at an EU meeting who planned to attend the sold-out event. I was the only one who raised my hand. My youngest daughter and I had a really enjoyable evening, which the compère concluded with Atatürk's often-repeated quotation: 'Peace at home, peace in the world'. I could not but marvel throughout the evening at how the woman next to me in the VIP arena could bear the stifling heat in her full headscarf and traditional coat from shoulder to ankle.

The quest to join the EU has given Turkey a sense of common destiny. 'We consider ourselves both European and Asian and view this duality to be an asset,' stated former Foreign Minister Cem before a crucial EU summit in 1997.[1] He emphasized that Turkey had lived for seven hundred years of its history in Europe and as a European power.

In a recent survey on nationalism, people were questioned as to where they felt they most belonged[2]. 'Turkey' was the answer given by the majority. Religion was found by the respondents to be the most indispensable characteristic of Turkey's identity during the EU membership process.

---

1. Ismail Cem, *For EU, an Issue of Identity and Vision*, IHT, November 1997.
2. Cüneyt Ülsever on a survey by Bilgi University, Infakto Research Workshop, for 'Tempo', *Turkish Daily News*, 11 April 2006.

The 2004 green light to start EU membership negotiations gave a tremendous boost to Turkish self-image. It confirmed Turkey's European identity and sense of belonging. Atatürk's forceful European quest, initiated more than seventy years earlier, had reached a new level. The Erdoğan government's strenuous reform efforts were acknowledged and rewarded by the EU.

The controversial and emotional debate on Turkish identity will remain in the spotlight for a number of reasons. The unfolding EU process is one. The increasing divide between the secular establishment and the Islamic-rooted government is another. The uncertainty of the future of neighbouring Iraq and the growing assertiveness and impatience among its Kurds is an additional contributing factor to the burning issue of Turkish identity. This will not change any time soon.

TWO

Turkey in the Waiting Room of the European Union

Turkey's quest to join Europe goes back a long way. Paradoxically, Atatürk and the other founding leaders of modern Turkey came from the battlefields of the Western invasion forces in the 1920s and created a new secular republic inspired by Western models. The new legal system was based on Swiss and Italian legislation. Secularism replaced Islam as the official, state ethos. The Latin alphabet was introduced after the swift abolition of the Arabic alphabet; all of which exemplifies the reach of Western influences in the process of making modern Turkey. 'This bears witness to our pragmatic sense, but also to Turkey's ability to overlook past grievances and to create the future,' argued then Foreign Minister Cem in a speech to his EU colleagues in 1999.[1]

World War II and beyond

During World War II, Turkey pursued a cautious policy that it labelled 'active neutrality', which kept it out of the war almost until

---

1.   Ismail Cem, *Turkey in the New Century*, Rustem Publishing, 2001, p. 201.

the very end. By joining the Allies in February 1945, Turkey qualified to become one of the founding members of the United Nations together with the victorious world powers.

Turkey never hesitated to join what were essentially Western alliances and institutions. Membership of the Organization for Economic Cooperation and Development (OECD) and the Council of Europe followed in 1949. The beginning of the cold war at that time brought greater geo-strategic importance to Turkey, being a frontline state to the Soviet Union. That, combined with fighting alongside US forces in the Korean War, paved the way for Turkish NATO membership in 1952. Greece joined the nineteen-member security pact simultaneously. Turkey's Western credentials were further strengthened in the mid-1950s when it took France's side in the eight-year-long war of independence in Muslim Algeria, an act for which President Özal emotionally apologized to the Algerian people decades later.

Turkey's efforts to integrate with Europe have been made on and off since 1949. These efforts reflect long-held national aspirations as well as a desire to secure greater welfare and security. When Greece applied for associate EEC (as the EU was then known) membership in 1959, it sent shock waves through Ankara. Two weeks later, on 31 July, Turkey followed suit. Turkish Prime Minister Menderes argued that Turkey could under no circumstances sit back and watch Greece become a member. 'What can they do that we cannot?' was his rhetorical argument when questions were raised about whether Turkey really was in a position to enter into economic relations with the newly founded, six-member EEC. But Turkish commitment to negotiations was lacklustre at the time. It would be another twenty-eight years before Turkey applied for full membership.

Less than a year after Turkey applied for associate membership, the political landscape changed dramatically and the change ended in tragedy. Political tension related to other issues, coupled with discontent within the army resulted in a military coup in September

1960, ending a decade of power for the once popular Democrat Party. Modern Turkey's first period of parliamentary democracy came to an abrupt and violent end after only ten years. Prime Minister Menderes, together with his foreign and finance ministers, was hanged in September 1961. Appeals from Queen Elizabeth, President Kennedy and other heads of state around the world to spare their lives were futile. In Turkey many were horrified, including a seven-year-old boy whose sadness turned into an attraction to politics. His name was Tayyip Erdoğan.

The Ankara agreement

The military coup in 1960 delayed the Turkey–EEC negotiations. It was only two years after Greece became an associate member that Turkey concluded the 'Ankara agreement' with the EEC. The treaty between the two parties was signed on 12 September 1963. This Association Agreement envisaged an eventual membership for Turkey in the EEC. From then on Turkey was an EEC partner and set itself full membership as a target. The economic policy and political choices made by Turkey from then on were influenced by the membership bid. Turkey felt it should no longer be necessary to have to prove over and over again that it was a European country.

At the time of the signing, the EEC Commissioner Walter Hallstein said: 'Today we are witnessing a historic event. Turkey belongs in Europe. Here lies the significance of this event. This is an expression of reality rather than a summarized geographical fact or the historical events of the past few centuries'.[1] Turkey took this view, as expressed by the Commissioner, to be the official EEC policy on Turkey. Time would prove that it was not quite so simple.

The Ankara agreement gave structure to relations between Turkey and the EEC, and eventually to those with the European Community (EC) and the EU. But these relations did not develop smoothly.

---

1.   Onur Öymen, *Turkish Challenge*, Cambridge University Press, 2000, pp. 219–235.

Tensions were frequent, especially during the late 1970s, late 1980s and throughout the 1990s.

Four decades on a bumpy road: Troubled European neighbourhood and domestic instability

Despite being an associate member Turkey was treated somewhat as a distant relative of the EEC during the next four decades. Europe's reluctance to embrace Turkey was to a large extent due to the political instability and human rights violations within Turkey itself. Relations with Greece, historically an adversary, and the closely linked Cyprus question were other crucial hurdles to be overcome on Turkey's European odyssey.

Relations with Greece and Cyprus

Some historians believe that the rivalry between what are today Greece, Cyprus and Turkey goes back three thousand years to the Trojan wars. Only empires such as the Byzantine and the Ottoman managed to uphold peace. This historical competition has had lasting and far-reaching effects on Turkey's long quest to join the EU.

Cyprus has been divided ever since 1974 when the Turkish army invaded the tiny island to pre-empt a union (*enosis*) between Cyprus and Greece. It was also to protect the Turkish-speaking minority. Since its independence from Britain in 1960, Cyprus had suffered from recurrent ethnic conflicts between the Greek Cypriots and the Turkish Cypriots.

When Britain – as one of the guarantors of an independent Cyprus – refused Turkey's appeal to intervene and stop the attempts to unify Cyprus with Greece, Prime Minister Ecevit swiftly ordered a military invasion on 20 July 1974. The invasion astonished and shocked the world. After more than two decades as a loyal and reliable NATO-ally, Turkey's Western credentials were brought into question.

Cyprus applied for EC membership in 1962, the same year as

Britain, its primary trading partner. When the British EC application was rejected by France during de Gaulle's presidency, Cyprus's membership bid was put on hold. It was only when Charles de Gaulle departed from power that Britain could eventually join the EEC in 1974, in its first drive for enlargement.

Turkey's European integration process and the planned Customs Union came to a halt after the Cyprus crises in 1974. A stalemate followed, and the situation deteriorated further with the proclamation of the self-declared Turkish Republic of Northern Cyprus in 1983. The Republic's undisputed leader Rauf Denktaş enjoyed considerable power and respect in mainland Turkey, which was the sole country to recognize it. Turkish influence on northern Cyprus was omnipresent in every aspect of life; politically, economically and militarily.

The new EC member state Greece, which joined in 1981, demanded a revival of Cyprus's EC integration efforts. The Greek Cypriots applied for membership, on behalf of the whole island, in 1990. It took the EU Commission three whole years to give its formal views (*avis*), where reservations were expressed against allowing accession talks for Cyprus before a solution was found to the divided island. A breakthrough for Cyprus came at an EU summit on Corfu in 1994. The EU leaders – there were ten of them at the time – declared their intention to accept Cyprus as an EU member even if no solution were found to the conflict. A historical compromise was reached the following year. Cyprus was given a date to start membership talks and Greece withdrew its veto against an EU–Turkish Customs Union.

The EU's decision to offer membership to Cyprus provided momentum for the parties to resolve their long-standing dispute. While the UN remained in charge of the peace efforts there were no longer any doubts that Turkey's EU membership ambition was part of the Cyprus equation. Turkey thus became an important piece of the puzzle during the EU's fifth drive for enlargement, the largest in its history.

Turkey's struggle with political instability

Prime Minister Ecevit failed to capitalize on his enormous popularity following his ordering of the Cyprus invasion. He was outmanoeuvred by his conservative rival Süleyman Demirel. The two of them took turns holding the reins of power during the turbulent 1970s, which were marred by political violence and an economy in complete disarray.

Until the mid-1970s Turkey and Greece kept in step on their respective paths towards the EEC. But as Greece rapidly approached membership by signing its accession treaty in 1979, Turkey was tripping up. Leftist Ecevit, a fervent supporter of the Third World, claimed that the agreements with the EEC had hindered development in Turkey. He promised that his government would make sure it would not be crushed by the EEC.[1] Turkey's request for eight billion US dollars in aid and credits from the EEC was viewed as a vastly exaggerated claim. The request was not surprisingly rejected in Brussels.

This caused a major setback in the Turkish membership bid. Some believe that it was the sheltered Turkish industries, dominated by a handful of influential families in Istanbul, which contributed to the government's decision to demand an exaggerated price tag. The Turkish monopolies, existing since the time of Atatürk, were not yet ready to take on open market competition from the EEC.

Soon afterwards, in 1980, there were deliberations about Turkey applying for full membership. However, these were contested domestically. When the foreign minister, Hayrettin Erkmen, concerned over the imminent Greek accession, publicly stated that a Turkish application would be made soon, he was forced to resign. The no-confidence vote against the foreign minister was orchestrated by Bülent Ecevit and Necmettin Erbakan (who later became Turkey's first Islamic prime minister).

The military coup in September 1980, preceded by 5,000 casualties

1.   A. Mango, *Turks of Today*, p. 78.

due to political violence, brought an immediate halt to the debate on whether or not it was time to apply for membership. Relations between Turkey and the EEC cooled off considerably while political parties were banned and leading politicians and trade unionists arrested. A restricted new Constitution was adopted in 1983, which gave the military strong influence.

Restarting the reform process

The European integration process restarted in the same year, spearheaded by the liberal Turgut Özal, a fifty-four-year-old engineer and a protégé of President Demirel. Özal, a practising Muslim of Kurdish origin, became leader of the 'Motherland Party' (ANAP). He became prime minister only a year after his party was established. He engaged Turkey in substantial economic reforms. A period of rapid and liberal economic development followed. Turkey was getting ready to apply for full European Community membership.

Turkey was facing a 'long, narrow, steep and stony road ahead'. These were the words of Prime Minister Özal on 14 April 1987, when the milestone application was handed in. Never before had a Turkish leader tackled the EC process with such purposefulness and realism. It was no coincidence that Özal was later often described by top EU officials as the biggest reformist after Atatürk. These compliments were expressed a decade after – by then President – Özal's untimely death in 1993.

After two and a half years, the EC gave its formal reply to Turkey's application: Turkey was eligible for full membership. However, the time was not viewed as ripe to launch membership talks. There were political deficiencies with improvements needed in democracy and human rights. Excessively high protectionism and structural differences between the EC and Turkey in industry and agriculture were other reasons given by the EC Commission. The Cyprus issue and Greek–Turkish relations were also major factors.

There were disappointment and a sense of double standards

in Turkey. Criticism of Turkey's democracy was a sensitive point. While Turkey had had a multi-party system since 1946, some of the other applicant countries had recently emerged from long periods of dictatorship. Spain and Portugal had only benefited from democracy for three years when the EU Commission made its decision on these two applications in 1978, praising their development into democracies. However, it took another eight years for the two Iberian countries to become members.

Democracy and human rights

While Turkey was making steady economic progress, serious problems were brewing in the southeast of the country. The Kurdish separatist party, the PKK, began its insurgency in 1984. The next fifteen years were marred by a brutal civil war between the Turkish army and the Marxist–Leninist PKK. The war left more than 30,000 people dead. Hundreds of thousands of people had to leave their villages – for fear or by force – and move to cities. Human rights abuses were widespread and Turkey was faced with harsh criticism in the European Parliament, Council of Europe and in bilateral contacts.[1] Many of the allegations of human rights abuses were angrily denied by consecutive Turkish governments, viewing their rejections as valid and a justified part of the struggle against terrorist activities.

There was a general feeling of unjust and exaggerated criticism. Former Foreign Minister Ismail Cem (who was also a writer and journalist) believed that there was a link between the decline of Turkey's strategic value after the cold war and growing Western criticism of Turkey's weaknesses in democracy and human rights. Mr Cem wrote:

> The Council of Europe turned Turkey into a target for taking pot-shots at. At a time when Turkey was actually making progress towards more democracy, the same West that had

---

1.   See chapter 6 on the Kurdish question.

once regarded all the country's faults as normal had suddenly
mutated into evangelists of human rights and democracy – at
least where Turkey was concerned.

The sudden change with which Turkey was confronted at
the end of the cold war brought a mixture of strong reactions.
A sense of shock was followed by alienation and strong
feelings of isolation and insecurity.[1]

Despite ongoing controversies on human rights issues, lengthy
negotiations took place on a customs union, resulting in an agreement
in 1990. An important benchmark in EU–Turkish relations was
achieved when the Customs Union finally came into effect on 31
December 1995.

A twist of irony brought in the ardently anti-EU Necmettin
Erbakan as the new prime minister shortly thereafter. He had strongly
criticized Turkey's EU membership application in 1987. Turkey would
not benefit either politically or economically from membership, he
believed. Erbakan, who was the country's first Islamic prime minister,
had declared his preference to cooperate with other Muslim countries
and not the EU, which he described as a 'Christian organization'. 'Our
history is a history of 1,500 years of conflict between the European
and Islamic cultures.'[2] However, his aversion to EU membership and
the brand new Customs Union changed. Once his 'Welfare Party'
entered into a coalition government, headed by Erbakan, in July 1996,
there was a reversal of policy in a number of different areas, not only
relating to Europe. His enthusiasm for Islamic regimes in countries
like Iran and Libya pushed the limits of Turkey's secular system too
far. It contributed to him being ousted from power by the military
and the establishment after only one year. Turkey had had its first
'soft' postmodern coup.

---

1. I. Cem, *Turkey in the New Century*, pp. 34–35.
2. Elisabeth Özdalga, *Erbakan: Democracy for the Sake of Power*, Lexington Books,
    p. 136.

Crisis after Luxembourg summit

In late 1997, Erbakan's conservative, pro-EU successor Mesut Yilmaz was faced with the deepest crisis so far between the EU and Turkey. When Turkey was excluded from being declared a candidate country at the EU summit in Luxembourg in December 1997, political dialogue with the EU was severed. Simply being referred to as an applicant country and not receiving candidate status was not acceptable to the Turkish government. A period of limited contact followed. It had been a unanimous decision by the fifteen EU leaders not to grant Turkey candidate status. Despite this, there remained lingering bitterness among some Turkish top officials towards Luxembourg – as host and head of the rotating EU presidency in late 1997 – for some years.

Breakthrough against the PKK

A rainbow coalition of left to right parties took power. Suddenly Turkey was faced with rock bottom relations with Greece when the PKK leader Öcalan turned out to be hiding in the Greek embassy in Kenya. His capture and return to imprisonment in Turkey in early 1999 was a major breakthrough in the civil war. Öcalan's renunciation of violence and the PKK's commitment to transform itself into a political organization in August 1999 was a turning point. Fifteen years of devastating civil war had finally come to an end.

U-turn in Turkish–Greek relations

On 17 August 1999, a devastating earthquake outside Istanbul took at least 20,000 lives. The earthquake brought a rapid humanitarian response. While the Turkish army was criticized for inefficiency in mobilizing rescue efforts, international help was quickly in place. Greece was one of the first countries to assist its neighbour. When Greece was hit by an earthquake a few weeks later, Turkey reciprocated. This paved the way for a *rapprochement* between the two long-standing adversaries.

The Turkish foreign minister Cem and his Greek counterpart George Papandreous initiated and embarked on the successful 'taverna diplomacy' which resulted in gradually improved bilateral relations. A newfound *modus vivendi* had been established. With Greece being an EU member and Turkey wanting to become one, this was an important turning point.

I was always astonished at how many Turks that I met were personally affected by the earthquake. Many Turkish diplomats grew up around Istanbul and some that I knew well had relatives who died when their improperly built apartment blocks collapsed. Often the massive earthquake was referred to as a new starting point in Turkey's relations with Greece. One of my Turkish colleagues lost both her parents in the earthquake. She only told me that after we had worked closely together on various business projects for a few years. I often found friends and colleagues in Turkey carrying deep grief with such impressive stoicism and resilience. There was never any dwelling on why it had to happen to their loved ones. It was rather a quiet acceptance of a fate beyond their control, perhaps thanks to their Muslim faith.

With this unexpected U-turn in Turkish–Greek relations, Turkey's chances of making progress in its EU bid looked more promising than ever before. Expectations were rising. Turkish candidate country status seemed to be within reach. Almost four decades in the EU's waiting room – by far the longest wait in EU history – appeared to be coming to an end.

THREE

Changing EU–Turkish Relations, 1999–2007

A watershed in EU–Turkish relations took place when Turkey was granted EU candidate status in the Finnish capital Helsinki just before Christmas 1999. The fifteen EU leaders declared that 'Turkey is a candidate state destined to join the Union on the basis of the same criteria applied to the other candidate states'. After forty years the longest waiting applicant country was allowed to leave the EU's waiting room. Turkey had finally become an official EU candidate country.

The decision in Helsinki was in the end unanimous, but it was not an easy one for Sweden, which through its Foreign Minister Anna Lindh passionately championed the cause of human rights in Turkey. The death penalty, torture and lack of cultural rights for the Kurds were some of the problems which were still unresolved. Turkey felt unfairly singled out by the young and dynamic cabinet minister, who was tipped to become the next prime minister of Sweden.

Anna Lindh's vocal human rights position consequently evoked strong resentment in many Turkish circles. Prime Minister Ecevit replied to her once, irritated, via a newspaper: 'We are enacting important laws, what else does Sweden want? Criticizing Turkey has become a jingle for the West.'[1] At that time, Ecevit was trying to keep one of his coalition partners in the government, the ultra-right-wing 'Nationalist Action Party', MHP. It had committed itself to keeping the death penalty as one of its electoral promises only a few months previously.

When Anna Lindh's life suddenly came to a brutal end four years later, the AK Party government was quick to praise her memory and her commitment to human rights. As a strong defender of human rights in Turkey, she was no longer dismissed as an 'enemy of Turkey' nor was she viewed as an obstacle on Turkey's path towards an EU accession. I was struck by the sentiments expressed by a Turkish general as well as by a leading Kurdish intellectual, who I met in Ankara only an hour after the stabbing of Anna Lindh in a department store in Stockholm. Both had already picked up information of the attack and were deeply concerned. Not only as to whether or not she would survive but also whether the attacker was an immigrant, fearing a backlash against Turkey if it had been a Muslim, which in fact turned out not to be the case. Mijailo Mijailovic, who was later sentenced to life for the murder, comes from Serbia, a mainly Christian country.

The reactions of concern and widespread grief in Turkey following the death of Anna Lindh were a reflection of how much Turkey had changed in a few years. A more self-critical and open-minded mentality was starting to take root. There was a willingness to change and to bring about reforms. This new state of mind facilitated the EU process considerably. But there were many crucial external factors beyond Turkey's control, which stirred up winds of change. That included two natural disasters and a redrawing of the whole European political landscape.

Leading up to the EU summit in Helsinki

Political liberalization in Turkey had not improved much from the

---

1.   Daily newspaper *Milliyet*, 23 September 1999.

time of the frozen top-level EU–Turkish dialogue in 1997 to the EU summit in Helsinki two years later. This meant that during this period little progress was made towards meeting the EU's political conditions for improved democracy and enhanced respect for human rights. The most important domestic factor enabling change was the capture of the PKK leader Abdullah Öcalan. It brought a gradual end to the long civil war. Draconian security measures could be revised. Suddenly, there was potential for improvement to the human rights situation as the EU summit in Helsinki approached. The breakthrough in relations between Turkey and Greece, following two consecutive earthquakes, further helped to brighten the picture.

When Tony Blair led the Labour Party to its biggest general election victory ever in May 1997, Turkey gained a vocal supporter of its EU ambitions in a key European capital. Another change of government a year later, this time in Germany, also benefited Turkey's EU quest. Chancellor Gerhard Schröder, upon taking power in 1998, took a positive stand on Turkey becoming a fully-fledged EU member in the future, unlike his Christian Democratic predecessor, former Chancellor Kohl. The substantial community of almost three million Turks living in Germany helped underpin this stand. They had become a political factor too big to be overlooked. With the EU's largest country and biggest budgetary contributor – Germany – now on its side, Turkey's EU chances were significantly enhanced. Jacques Chirac, president of France between 1995–2006, was another key European leader sympathetic to future Turkish membership despite strong opposition within his own party. His successor Nicolas Sarkozy took a completely different position. As one of the very few foreign policy issues in the French presidential campaign in spring 2007, Mr Sarkozy argued that Turkey does not belong in the EU. That position has been frequently repeated since Sarkozy took office as France's president.

The end of the cold war in the early 1990s changed the political landscape of Europe. It also changed Turkey's role as a key strategic partner within NATO and flank outpost against the Soviet Union. Turkey's geopolitical importance was reduced, although not for long. During the 1991 Gulf War, the US received wholehearted support from the Turkish president, Özal, who thus reasserted his role as a statesman vis-à-vis the West.

During the Clinton administration (1993–2001) active support was given to Turkish EU membership. Strategic reasons were emphasized, in particular during the late 1990s when EU–Turkey relations were frosty following the 1997 EU summit in Luxembourg. While addressing the Turkish Parliament during a visit to Turkey in November 1999, Bill Clinton stated that 'our vision of a Europe that is undivided, democratic and at peace for the first time in all of history will never be complete unless and until it embraces Turkey'. This unequivocal statement by the US president was made only a few weeks before the crucial EU summit in Helsinki. Clinton's visit is still talked about in glowing terms by many in Ankara, including the staff at the Hilton hotel, whom he personally thanked one by one during his stay there with his wife Hillary.

Around the same time, in November 1999, the newly appointed president of the EU Commission, Romano Prodi, gave reassurances to Turkey. The former Italian professor promised that there was no chance that the Helsinki summit would bring a repeat of what had happened in Luxembourg two years earlier.

Before the Helsinki summit, efforts intensified as Turkey tried to reach a solution to the more than thirty-year-long Cyprus conflict. Although the EU plays a subsumed role to the United Nations, its impact has increased substantially over the years, especially after the Cyprus EU membership became more imminent, i.e. after 1998. In early December 1999, UN-led 'proximity talks' on Cyprus were held in New York. The aim was to bring the Greek and Turkish Cypriot leaders to engage in direct negotiations for a comprehensive solution. Expectations were raised that the two sides, encouraged by a carrot in the form of future EU membership, would this time find a way to reunite the island. These talks, launched only a week before the gathering of the EU leaders in Helsinki, contributed towards creating a promising pre-summit atmosphere.

A crucial turning point in EU–Turkish relations

Leading up to the summit, Prime Minister Ecevit expressed concern over Turkey's strategic interest. The Cyprus issue and the longstanding maritime dispute with Greece over the Aegean Sea resurfaced. 'EU membership is a top priority for Turkey but not an obsession,' declared Foreign Minister Cem.[1] Ecevit's eight-month-old coalition government disagreed on whether to execute the captured PKK leader or wait for the ruling of the Strasbourg-based Human Rights Court. By waiting and thus keeping the moratorium on the death penalty, Turkey enhanced its chances of a favourable outcome in Helsinki. But the human rights situation remained gloomy. An attack against the office of the Human Rights Association in Ankara[2] illustrated the precarious situation that the few existing human rights organizations worked in. Its chairman, Hüsnü Öndül, was beaten and documents destroyed while uniformed police idly stood by.

During the EU summit on 10–11 December 1999, the newly appointed EU Foreign Policy Chief Javier Solana and EU Commissioner for enlargement Günther Verheugen suddenly had to leave Helsinki and fly to Ankara. Prime Minister Ecevit needed to be persuaded during the night of 10 December to agree to the text. A deal was not yet done. To accept that there was no requirement to solve the Cyprus issue before Cyprus was accepted as an EU member was a bitter pill to swallow for Turkey. So was the EU decision that the Aegean dispute, if not solved by 2004, would be referred to the International Court of Justice (ICJ).

But the following morning, Ecevit had given his consent and

---

1. Written statement on the EU issued by the Ministry of Foreign Affairs, 30 November 1999.
2. On 25 November 1999.

arrived in Helsinki in time for the European Council welcoming 'recent positive developments in Turkey' and making history by declaring that 'Turkey is a candidate State destined to join the Union on the basis of the same criteria as applied to other candidate States'. A historic watershed in EU–Turkish relations had been reached.

The reactions in Turkey were mainly positive. The government stressed the importance of the promise that Turkey 'will be treated on an equal footing with the other candidates' and that 'the door has been opened without any preconditions for Turkey's full membership'. But in a written statement the prime minister refused to accept that the Aegean dispute should be referred to the International Court.[1]

The Turkish media welcomed the historic decision with headlines such as 'Turkey is in the EU family', 'The meeting of the century' and 'First Muslim candidate country nominated'.[2] The Istanbul stock market rejoiced and, as a result, increased an incredible 10.9 per cent in a single day.

Turkey had achieved status as a candidate country but there was still a long way to go before membership talks could start. First the EU's political criteria had to be met. They were laid down by the EU leaders at a summit in Copenhagen in 1993 and consequently referred to as the Copenhagen Criteria. Candidate countries must have achieved 'stability of institutions guaranteeing democracy, the rule of law, human rights and respect for and protection of minorities' before membership talks could commence. Turkey was not even near to having fulfilled these political criteria. Widespread doubts within the EU were lingering as to whether Turkey would ever be able to do so.

EU candidature achieved: What next?

EU candidate status brought confirmation once and for all of Turkey's European identity. The psychological effect was important, something that might be difficult to fully comprehend in the West.

1. Press statement by Prime Minister Ecevit, 10 December 1999.
2. Turkish Daily News, Milliyet, Hürriyet.

A new confidence was noticeable. Prime Minister Ecevit predicted that Turkey could become a member as early as 2004 while Foreign Minister Cem was more restrained in his optimism. Euphoria certainly prevailed in the first few months of 2000 following the EU summit.

When a new president of the republic was elected in spring 2000 the symbolism was obvious. Ahmet Necdet Sezer was the country's first president with no political or military background. During Sezer's time as a top jurist, he was committed to democratization and focusing on the individual rather than the state. His appointment as Turkey's tenth president was viewed as another sign of commitment to the EU reform process. Things looked promising for Turkey and its pledges to change.

A new openness followed. The Kurdish issue was discussed in a fresh way, helped by rapidly decreasing killings in the conflict between the separatist PKK and the army. The widespread use of torture was researched and highlighted by Parliament in an unprecedented way. Nevertheless, the hopes of a take-off for the reform process never materialized in the aftermath of the historic Helsinki meeting. A devastating economic crisis in early 2001 and a weakened government coalition meant that many of the draft reforms never left the shelves. During the first year and a half following the grant of EU candidate status, little changed.

It would take another three years before a new major turning point occurred in EU–Turkish relations. In the meantime, several momentous events helped shape Turkey. The 9/11 terror attacks in the US turned Turkey – as a democratic Muslim society – into a role model. The EU reform process was suddenly rejuvenated under the Ecevit government. The general election in 2002 brought an unexpected pro-Islamic, single majority government into power with EU membership as its top priority. Meanwhile, a war in neighbouring Iraq was rapidly approaching with potential dire consequences for Turkey. Consequently, the political agenda in Turkey was brimming with critical issues in urgent need of being addressed. But moving forward in the EU accession process remained a top priority.

Arriving in Ankara

My first arrival in Ankara in autumn 2001 coincided with a flurry of unexpected EU activity. I had spent the previous seven years working on human rights questions in Geneva and later as ambassador in Lebanon. I expected my upcoming years in Turkey to be challenging and sometimes tough. Like most of my EU colleagues I never anticipated that Turkey's reforms would suddenly get off to a flying start. Fortunately, I was wrong.

I could only formally take up my posting as ambassador after presenting my letter of credentials. This consisted of a signed letter from the Swedish King Carl XVI Gustaf to President Sezer. Receiving an appointment at the Presidential Palace, perched on a crest of the Anatolian plateau, is usually based on strict reciprocity. If the Turkish ambassador in one host country gets a meeting with the head of state after a few weeks, which is usually the norm, this means that President Sezer would receive the foreign envoy after exactly the same amount of time. To me, this meant less than two weeks of waiting before officially taking up my duties in Turkey.

I was informed that spouses were welcome to attend the presidential ceremony, which is not always the case in many countries. My husband, being English and a master of small talk, unlike many Swedes, made sure there was no awkward silence while waiting for the formal ceremony to start. The president and his entourage were clearly fascinated at meeting the only male spouse to a foreign ambassador at the time. No one asked what my husband was doing, assuming he had followed me to my new posting. Later on, many were amazed learning about his long-distance commute between his work in Geneva and family in Ankara.

During the traditional tête-à-tête meeting following the handing over of my credentials, the president focused more on bilateral relations than the EU process. Combating the PKK is the most important, he stated. Sweden must do more to fight the terrorist organization. (Sweden has many immigrants originating from Kurdish areas in Turkey.) The president expressed his hope that I, during my posting, would be able to contribute to a different and more positive image of Turkey in the Swedish media. 'Too often it is unbalanced and full of mistakes.' I replied that it would be incorrect to try to influence journalists' work while referring to the importance of protecting freedom of the press. The president clarified that much is due to a lack of knowledge and therefore something I, as an ambassador, could help remedy.

When I returned to the Presidential Palace four years later to bid my formal farewell it was apparent how much water had flowed under the bridge. Comparing my first and last meetings with President Sezer, it was astounding how our bilateral relations had improved as a result of the successful EU reform process. I received a signed, silver-framed photo of the president as a farewell gift.

Reforms were set in motion in October 2001 when Parliament adopted a package of amendments to the 1982 Constitution. They were pushed through Parliament with a surprisingly large majority and great speed. The changes narrowed the grounds for limiting fundamental rights and freedoms, but still left major shortcomings, for instance when it came to freedom of expression. The thirty-seven Constitutional amendments were mainly a significant manifestation of Turkey's commitment to making progress. Among the reforms carried out by the left–right Ecevit government, limiting the use of capital punishment received most attention, although the EU continued to demand complete abolition.

At the time, Amnesty International was banned in the country. After much EU lobbying Amnesty was finally allowed to open an office in Ankara during spring 2002. A couple of years later its London-based Secretary General, Irene Khan, paid a visit. A reception in her honour, which I hosted, was attended by the AK Party minister of justice, Cemil Çiçek. His presence was an illustration of how dramatically attitudes had changed in a relatively short time.

EU report became a national obsession

The EU Commission had started to report regularly to the EU leaders on Turkey's progress, as well as on all the other candidate countries. The first fully-fledged Regular Report for Turkey was presented to the European Council Summit in Nice in December 2000. The release of this report in early October every year became something of a national obsession. Although the fascination started to fade as opposition to the Turkish bid grew within the EU.

The Turkish authorities and media usually managed to get hold of copies of the report shortly before the publication in Brussels, unlike the ambassadors from EU member states in Ankara. We usually had to wait for the official release of the approximately 140-page report. Turkish journalists, in search of comments and explanations from EU diplomats, always had a problem really believing that we, EU ambassadors, had had no preview of the full report, which was drafted in Ankara by the local EU Commission's delegation and later finalized in Brussels. That was embarrassing and on my part, at least, not for lack of trying. The widespread fascination for the bureaucratic and substantial report helped to create a positive momentum. Its dry, detailed writing boosted the reform process.

Turkey's progress was welcomed by the European Council, which met during the Belgian phase of the rotating EU Presidency in Laeken in December 2001. The positive development 'brought forward the prospect of opening of accession negotiations with Turkey,' declared the EU leaders. The statement was positively received in Turkey. It was viewed as a small but important step forward in the EU process. Attention was rapidly moving towards achieving a firm date when EU membership talks could start.

Although the reforms had widespread support in Parliament and among the public, contradictory forces were at work below the surface. Traditionalists with strong nationalistic sentiments feared or mistrusted the EU's real intentions. They stood against the reformists, who increasingly lobbied for one, single thing; a date for Turkey, with the Turkish industrialists' and businessmen's association, Tüsiad, taking the lead.

'The only way the EU can positively support the reform process is by giving Turkey a date to start membership negotiations.' That message was constantly repeated to me and others representing the EU or an EU country by Turks from all walks of life. The message came from Turkish colleagues in the Foreign Ministry and the EU General Secretariat at the prime minister's office, parliamentarians, many human rights defenders and non-governmental organizations across the country. The business sector was also actively supporting the bid for a date.

The passion and hopes attached to EU membership were simply astonishing during the period 2002–5, which is sometimes described as the 'golden era'. They were constant reminders to me that the EU was a strong catalyst and promoter of freedom and democracy rather than an anonymous Brussels-based bureaucratic machine, as its opponents like to portray it.

Fervour preceded EU summits

Turkey's relations with the EU revolved around the EU summit meetings held every six months. Reforms were pursued with fervour and so was the determination to have them explicitly acknowledged in summit statements by the EU leaders. As each summit approached, key policy measures were made while lobbying and speculation intensified. Many of Turkish television's forty or more channels had talk shows every night debating the EU process. Repeated opinion polls showed overwhelming support for membership, stronger than in any other of the then twenty-eight EU and candidate countries, with Romania as the only exception. To the average Mr Osman, the EU symbolized affluence and a better future.

The Copenhagen summit in December 2002 was the next step on Turkey's path towards joining the EU. An ambitious 'EU Action Plan' was launched by the government, supported by the president, the business sector and NGOs. In summer 2002, a new foreign minister, Sukru Sina Gürel, was appointed. He was widely known to be an EU sceptic. His appointment gave a mixed, if not confusing, signal as the huge campaign for a date to start membership talks intensified. Mr Gürel actively pursued the policy that it was now the EU's turn to deliver. Rarely was it mentioned by him or anyone else that the democratization process was good for Turkey. Instead, the emphasis was on the process being carried out as part of the EU application.

A German–French proposal outlined a decision on Turkey's date. It was suggested that a decision would be made in 2004 and that negotiations should start the following year. This was rejected by the new foreign minister of the ruling AK Party, Yaşar Yakiş. He argued that it was unacceptable that Turkey's fate would then be decided by twenty-five EU nations. It was never expressed explicitly, but it was the soon-to-be EU member Cyprus that deeply concerned the Turkish government. With the Cyprus issue still unresolved it was assumed that Cyprus would take an anti-Turkish stand.

Instead the new Turkish government pinned its hopes and ambitions for a starting date, if not in Copenhagen in late 2002, to the Greek EU presidency and the summit in Saloniki in June 2003. Thus the EU would have the time to fully evaluate the practical application of the new legislations. This would further enhance the friendly relations between Greece and Turkey, argued Foreign Minister Yakiş, a former diplomat with forty years' experience.

As the summit in Denmark approached, a few last minute and key policy decisions were made. The emergency rule in southeastern Turkey was lifted, for the first time since 1987.[1] Furthermore, the powerful National Security Council (NSC), consisting of the

---

1.   The two remaining provinces still under emergency rule were the regional centre Diyarbakir and Sirnak, near the Iraqi border.

country's top political and military leaders, changed its composition. Following EU demands to reduce the military's political influence, the number of civilians increased to eight representatives while the military retained five.

Despite all efforts and a massive lobbying campaign, no date was given to Turkey at the 2002 Copenhagen summit. Further reforms were deemed necessary. More time was needed to make sure the new laws were not merely on paper but actually implemented. The EU opted to act, not unexpectedly, along the lines of the German–French proposal. This meant that a commitment was given to 'open accession negotiations with Turkey without delay' if the summit in December 2004 decided that Turkey had fulfilled the Copenhagen political Criteria. The initial disappointment within the brand new AK Party Government soon turned into satisfaction. It was after all the first time in history when Turkey had a timetable, although conditional, for its EU membership talks. Yet another milestone had been reached in Turkey's EU quest.

Towards a breakthrough

A fierce determination to succeed with the reforms dominated in the ruling AK Party. An unprecedented campaign of change was pursued, most of the time supported by the main opposition party in Parliament. A sixth reform package was adopted by broad consensus in Parliament in the summer of 2003, despite opposition from the military and the president. Encouraging remarks from the EU boosted the process. Chancellor Schröder's and President Chirac's positive remarks on Turkey during the EU summit in Greece were well received in Ankara. It also showed that the EU was not a 'Christian Club', as one top official said to me.

The numbers of official visits to Turkey were skyrocketing, not only from Brussels but also from other European capitals. In addition, tourism was booming. When an American friend of mine was applying for a visa to come and visit Turkey for the first time, she was overwhelmed by the positive atmosphere at the Turkish consulate general in New York. 'Come back and tell us your impressions,' were the friendly parting words from the visa officer, which stunned her as a native New Yorker.

After two decades as the black sheep of the European family, Turkey was benefiting from people's accumulated desire to travel there. From the time that the EU gave a timetable to Turkey there was a rapid increase in visiting delegations. There was curiosity about the relatively unknown AK government with little previous experience of the EU. At my embassy the numbers of delegates doubled every year from 2002 onwards. Local and national politicians (including the first ever visit by a Swedish prime minister to Ankara in early 2004), journalists and trade unionists were among the many visitors.

The EU's enlargement with a record ten new members in May 2004 created a halo of success around it. This had a positive spillover effect on Turkey, as it was ambitiously pursuing the next stage in its EU relations.

Romance and reforms

Among my many and diverse duties as ambassador was performing civil marriages. My eleven-year-old daughter proudly announced to her friends that her mother was a vicar and an ambassador (in that order), despite my objections. As much as I enjoyed Ankara, it is definitely not a romantic city and it is, unlike Istanbul, off the beaten track. I was therefore always a bit surprised when couples chose to get married there. One middle-aged couple from a small town in Sweden, with no ties to Turkey, explained their reasons for choosing Ankara for their wedding ceremony. 'There are so many positive changes and reforms taking place here,' was their unexpected reply. I was impressed that the democratization of Turkey touched ordinary people's lives at the other edge of Europe.

The big democratic strides taken by Turkey were, however, threatened in November 2003. Two terrorist attacks in Istanbul against the British Consulate and synagogues killed more than fifty people. The British Consulate was destroyed by a massive car bomb, killing the top UK diplomat in Istanbul, Consul General Roger Short, and many others. People living nearby in central Istanbul first thought it was an earthquake. There were fears within the EU that the terrorist attacks would undermine the process towards more freedom and openness. It later turned out that that was not the case.

The Turkish Foreign Minister at the time, Mr Gül, accompanied by ten delegates, was visiting the Swedish Parliament on the morning of 20 November 2003 when urgent hand-delivered messages started to arrive. During a meeting with the Swedish Parliamentarian Committee on EU Affairs a second terror attack in Istanbul had been carried out. From early on, it was clear that there were many casualties and several hundred wounded. Foreign Minister Gül and his delegation were remarkably calm and quietly efficient. The meetings in Stockholm carried on without any major interruptions. The time of the departure of the government plane back to Ankara a few hours later remained unaltered. Watching how Abdullah Gül and his team were handling the crisis, I could not but think that those are the kind of people you would like to have next to you in the trenches.

Crucial movements on Cyprus and Kurdish issues

The EU process in Turkey was on an unprecedented roll in 2004, fuelled by widespread and robust parliamentary and popular support. Sweeping changes were transforming Turkey in what was described as a 'silent revolution'. New laws were geared to bring Turkey closer to the EU norms. Some taboos were broken along the way.

Complaints about changes without enough substance brought increased attention to the application of the new laws. The government, with a weakness for catchy labels, declared 2004 'the year of implementations'.

The significant shift in Turkish policy on Cyprus had a positive influence on the EU process. Prime Minister Erdoğan and his government were the first Turkish rulers to openly question and confront the status quo policy of the Turkish Cypriot leader Denktaş. 'No solution on Cyprus is no solution,' was the often-repeated statement by the Ankara government. Without its strong backing of the 'Kofi Annan Plan', it is unlikely that the Turkish Cypriots would have supported it as they did in the referendum in spring 2004. But the Greek Cypriot rejection of the UN plan brought a hasty end to the growing optimism about reuniting the Mediterranean island. No solution could be reached in time for Cyprus as it joined the EU on 1 May 2004.

Other highly sensitive matters were being dealt with in a groundbreaking fashion. The state television and radio channels began broadcasting in Kurdish for the first time in history in June 2004. Some Kurdish-speaking people that I met complained that the programmes were too short and were often state propaganda films or nature programmes. They impatiently overlooked the importance of the historical principle that had been established.

The former Kurdish activist Leyla Zana was released from prison around the same time. Years of lobbying for Zana and her three fellow Kurdish parliamentarians by the Council of Europe and the EU could come to an end. Europe's most famous political prisoner was finally free. She publicly denounced violence as she was leaving the prison. Anything else would have been a catastrophe, undermining the credibility of all within the EU and elsewhere who had lobbied for her release. The news of Leyla Zana's release was broken to me by an excited Turkish journalist friend. He rang me while I was driving through the ancient city of Kirşehir in the heartland of Anatolia on a hot day in June 2004. He firmly believed this meant that Turkey had secured a date for accession talks.

At a small lunch with Leyla Zana a few weeks later, I found her lack of bitterness surprising as well as hopeful. We met in an almost empty fish restaurant in the outskirts of Ankara, surrounded by newly built high-rise apartment blocks. Her skin was strikingly pale and translucent, the result of a decade in prison without sunshine. She spoke with warmth about the many speeches that she had read in prison by Anna Lindh, who championed the cause of human rights for Kurds. Leyla Zana was visibly upset while talking about the sudden death of the Swedish foreign minister as well as that of Princess Diana.

Leyla Zana was never convicted of any violent crime, but for assisting terrorism. Softly spoken, petite and illiterate until adulthood, it was difficult to picture her as a serious threat. A few years later, on the eve of the general elections in July 2007, she called for the establishment of a Kurdistan federation within Turkey, confirming her position as a highly controversial politician.

The two almost consecutive decisions on broadcasting in Kurdish and a Turkish court freeing Leyla Zana resulted in euphoria. In no other country has potential EU membership aroused such passion. 'Two gigantic steps towards the EU' and 'No more excuses left for the EU' were some of the headlines in the biggest Turkish newspapers over the following days.

Towards securing the country's greatest ambitions

A trip to several cities in Turkey by the EU Commissioner for Enlargement Günther Verheugen in September 2004 was closely watched. The EU Commissioner's detailed knowledge of Turkey was impressive and his assertive style, I believed, inspired confidence in Turkey's EU position at a critical moment. Verheugen's trip was viewed by the government and other pro-EU forces as an important indicator of the EU's intentions at the upcoming summit in Brussels. But the visit was nearly overshadowed by the Turkish government's plan to criminalize adultery, which was met by an outcry within the EU as well as in Turkey. The proposal was subsequently dropped.

The EU Commission made a landmark decision when it recommended the start of negotiations between the EU and Turkey. The recommendation was declared in the highly anticipated 2004 Progress Report, which was released on 6 October. The Commission considered that Turkey had sufficiently fulfilled the political criteria for accession negotiations to be opened. But there was no assurance of a future membership. The accession talks would be 'an open-ended process whose outcome cannot be guaranteed beforehand,' the Commission stated. The date for the negotiations to start was left for the EU leaders to decide at the December 2004 summit.

As the crucial EU summit approached, tension in the domestic political climate was accelerated. Pressure increased on the government not to allow any concessions, particularly on Cyprus. The main opposition party, CHP, demanded in a parliamentary debate a joint declaration before the European Council meeting. It would have reduced the government's manoeuvring space and was rejected. The CHP was increasingly questioning the government's willingness to defend Turkey's honour and the nation's affairs of the heart.

More and more, the government was faced with criticism that the price was getting too high for a date to start membership talks, no matter how historic. Mistrust among the establishment for the government resurfaced. Meanwhile, the strong grass-roots support for the government kept growing, helped by a strong economy.

The atmosphere in Ankara leading up to the 2004 EU summit was charged. There were persistent rumours that Turkey would give a negative response to the European leaders, something the Dutch EU Presidency found highly unlikely. Nothing but the upcoming EU decision on Turkey was being discussed. As is so often the case in Turkey, the views were passionate and mostly black or white. 'We have historic hours ahead of us,' said an optimistic Erdoğan to the EU ambassadors at a lunch appointment two days ahead of the Brussels meeting.

Difficult discussions on Turkey dominated the two-day summit. EU was about to make one of the biggest decisions in its history. The key questions were discussed at a dinner with the twenty-five EU prime ministers on 16 December. First, an agreement was reached on a date. Negotiations with Turkey would open on 3 October 2005, as long as Turkey met some preconditions on Cyprus and on an amended Penal Code.

The Cyprus issue turned out to be the sticking point. Intense negotiations followed. There was a déjà vu situation with developments during the 1999 Helsinki summit. On the morning of the second day of the summit, the main opposition party in Turkey demanded that its government should immediately freeze negotiations with the EU. Meanwhile, left-wing parties demonstrated in Ankara against 'Turkey's submissiveness towards the EU'. After hours of brinkmanship and threats by the Turkish delegation to abruptly leave Brussels, a compromise was reached. Turkey committed to signing the 'Ankara protocol' before starting accession talks, extending the Customs Union agreement to all new EU members, including Cyprus.

The EU's decision was a turning point in European history. Strategic and economic relations were already well established. EU–Turkish relations were now, for the first time, moving towards full integration. Turkey had secured its greatest political ambitions. Although no guarantee was given of full membership, every previous country had received an offer to join after the membership talks.

Gloom leading up to membership talks

Before Turkey started its membership negotiations in October 2005, much had changed. The rejection of the EU Constitution by France and the Netherlands created uncertainty and pessimism within the EU as to how and when to proceed next. In Turkey, many people were surprised and confused that the Constitution had been rejected by two of the EU's founding members. Growing enlargement fatigue across Europe added further uncertainty and gloom to the Turkish EU bid.

But the upcoming autumn 2005 elections in Germany caused more concern in Turkey than the EU's institutional wrangle. Chancellor Schröder's unwavering support for Turkish EU ambitions meant a great deal, both politically and psychologically, in Turkey. There were no expectations in Ankara of Angela Merkel changing her views on Turkey if her party, the Christian Democrats, came to power in Germany. Its recommendation to offer Turkey 'a privileged partnership', rather than full membership, was well known in Ankara after several visits there by the then opposition leader. Other key European leaders, who were staunchly supportive of Turkey's EU application, were either leaving office or had already left; Tony Blair, Jacques Chirac, Silvio Berlusconi and Gerhard Schröder.

The negotiating rules were agreed during autumn 2005, setting the toughest conditions yet for an aspiring EU member. Among the provisions was a clause to stop the talks if Turkey persistently breached human rights laws or rule of law. If Turkey joined, other member states would be able to regulate Turkish immigration.

In Turkey progress was still being made during 2005 but at a slower pace. EU frustration was growing over Turkey's lacklustre performance on reforms and their implementation. Human rights violations were diminishing but the pace of reforms had definitely slowed down. The lack of progress concerning Cyprus was another source of deep dissatisfaction.

The appointment of Turkey's first EU chief negotiator, Ali Babacan, came after months of intense speculation and was met with general approval. The evening before the announcement he was attending a dinner at my residence. He was not yet aware of the next day's appointment, something which he confirmed to me almost two years later when I walked alongside the waterfront in Stockholm with him and his visiting delegation.

High-level visits from Sweden during the summer of 2005 by the then Speaker of Parliament, von Sydow, the future head of state, Crown Princess Victoria, and Trade Minister Östros, provided several opportunities to discuss with Turkey's new EU chief negotiator (who at thirty-eight was the youngest cabinet member). In his quietly confident way, he emphasized that the EU perspectives were long-term. He had noticed a changing mentality among Turks. Economic reasons were no longer the prime motivation for people wanting to join the EU, said Babacan, who was juggling his role with being minister of the economy at the same time. Instead the incentive was to achieve democratization and political stability.

'3 October will be the beginning of a new era,' Babacan said confidently in one of our meetings. The growing scepticism or opposition in EU countries, especially in France, Germany and Austria, to Turkish accession did not seem to seriously hamper him or his government's determination and long-term optimism. Prime Minister Erdoğan was equally convinced about the future EU prospects. 'Without any doubt, Turkey will become a member, whether it will take five, ten or fifteen years,' Erdoğan stressed at a meeting with EU ambassadors in Ankara in June 2005. It was a common trait among AK Party officials, I found, to take a significantly longer time perspective, well beyond the next election, compared with most Western politicians. This is a cultural difference which is often either overlooked or underestimated in Western Europe.

The launch of the negotiations in Brussels on 3 October 2005 was preceded by quite a painful process. Brinkmanship tactics, led by Austria, were used to seek to circumvent the mandate to start negotiations with further conditions. Skilful work by the British EU Presidency paved the way to the formal opening of membership negotiations. But it became increasingly clear that the Cyprus question would be the main controversy for the next few years. Ankara's lingering refusal during 2006 to allow Greek Cypriots to enter Turkish ports and airports contradicted an EU Customs Union protocol. It highlighted the obstacles ahead. Nevertheless, eight months after the formal opening of negotiations, the first chapter of Turkey's accession talks opened in June 2006, starting with the uncontroversial subjects of science and research. Negotiations followed in other relatively easy areas ('chapters') including industrial policy, statistics and financial control, but several contentious ones remain. In December 2006, the EU leaders decided to freeze eight chapters due to the EU's impasse with Turkey over Cyprus. Furthermore, no chapters would be closed until the deadlock was broken. The accession negotiations faced more obstacles when three key areas were blocked from being opened by France in June 2007.

After 2005, the momentum of political reform slowed. Implementation of reforms was uneven. Turkey developed an early pre-election mood. The AK Party had little manoeuvring space for concessions on crucial issues in the EU negotiations. Growing nationalism and reduced enthusiasm for the EU created new limitations but with the resounding success in the 2007 elections a robust resumption of the reform process is a real possibility. So is the prospect of a more self-confident and forward-looking EU as a result of the agreement on a Treaty. This approval by the twenty-seven EU leaders in December 2007 might reinvigorate the ambitious plans of continued enlargements of the Union, benefiting not only the western Balkans but also Turkey.

The solid optimism that Turkey will become an EU member in the future has eroded, not only among many Turks but also among its political leaders. The increasing resistance in key EU capitals towards a Turkish EU membership has clearly taken a toll. This became obvious at some meetings I had when visiting Ankara in December 2007 together with a top Swedish parliamentarian, Mr Lennmarker. In a small meeting in the presidential palace, the newly appointed President Gül did not hide from us his deep disappointment with the EU process. The commitment to reforms and an EU membership was still there but the strong conviction that it is attainable, which I have seen so often during the last five years, was less evident. The same attitude prevailed in a meeting with Ali Babacan, who succeeded Mr Gül as the foreign minister in autumn 2007 while maintaining the position as Turkey's chief EU negotiator.

The EU entry talks with Turkey are expected to last a decade. It will be a bumpy road ahead, especially with EU–Turkish relations being back at a perilous crossroads. But looking back on their past relations, there have been plenty of these, all of which have been overcome, one way or the other.

FOUR

Pro-Islamic Party Gained Power and Succeeded in Historic EU Breakthrough

It started out as any ordinary Sunday. Streets were quiet and shops closed. It was a day off, unlike in any other Muslim country in the region, where Friday is the day of rest. People were strolling to the election polls, which were mandatory but with only a symbolic fine for those skipping voting. It was 3 November 2002 and a general election had been held which would transform the course of Turkish history. It was held against the backdrop of one of Turkey's worst economic crises. Some of Turkey's best-known political leaders and their parties were facing the prospect of being wiped out in the election. It had been an unusually sunny and warm November day in Ankara, which had grown from a small hill town of 30,000 in the 1920s to a capital of more than four million people, located on the high and vast Anatolian plateau, where late autumn can be bitterly cold. Ankara was buzzing with the tide of democratic renewal.

I was spending the evening with Turkish friends, watching the TV coverage of the parliamentary election. We were flicking between the many different Turkish TV channels. The counting and analysis of the election results were impressive. More than thirty-one million votes were rapidly being accounted for. Ultra-modern graphics were flashing on the screen, illustrating the emerging and unexpected result, while political commentators were debating what the outcome would mean for Turkey's EU bid.

The election day turned out to be historic but the preceding campaign had been low-key and rather uneventful. Campaign buses for the various political parties, covered with huge pictures of their party leaders, were the most visible sign in Ankara of the upcoming election. Posters across the town were rather discreet and rarely featured slogans, mostly only party symbols. The quest to join the EU was therefore not prominent in the streets while it was discussed in daily, often heated, political debates in the media.

The only openly anti-EU stand was taken by the young media mogul and party leader Cem Uzan. With his media empire and political ambitions, he was sometimes compared to Italy's Silvio Berlusconi. Uzan's rabidly populist Youth Party (*Genç Partisi*) campaigned against EU membership as well as the presence in Turkey of the International Monetary Fund (IMF). Despite a hugely expensive campaign and plenty of media attention the party failed to get into Parliament. Some opponents claimed that the real driving force behind Uzan's candidature to become a member of parliament was to be granted immunity. He and his family had fought a legal battle for several years against massive fraud allegations.

The other main contenders were all nominally pro-EU, but in reality the picture was somewhat different and more complex. Some leading politicians were highly sceptical about a number of key reforms that were required to proceed in the EU process. Ensuring cultural rights for the Kurds was one of those required steps. This was widely viewed as a threat to the country's unity. Mistrust and fear of Turkey being divided along ethnic borders ran deep. It still does. One of the coalition partners in the government, the ultra-right-wing Nationalist Action Party (*Milliyetçi Hareket Partisi*; MHP), had distinctly ambivalent sentiments towards the political price Turkey had to pay for its EU ambitions. It viewed the election as a choice between those 'loving Brussels or Turkey'.

When the MHP's party leader, Dr Devlet Bahçeli, invited the EU ambassadors in Ankara to a dinner, the invitation was something of a surprise. The MHP election campaign had been fairly anti-EU. In addition, his party had demanded my expulsion from Turkey after a political controversy with Sweden on some human rights issues. The MHP's ultra-nationalistic rhetoric contributed to an escalation of the Turkish–Swedish controversy. Daily death threats against my daughter and myself were delivered for several weeks. Still, I believed Sweden should be represented at the dinner. The MHP was after all one of the parties in the government. However, I asked my deputy to attend. I was personally unwilling to accept a dinner invitation after the MHP's attempt within the government to declare me *persona non grata*. It turned out that I did not miss an interesting evening. The party leader, Devlet Bahçeli, never turned up to host his own dinner for the EU ambassadors. There was no reason given for his absence. My EU colleagues were left with some party officials. It certainly looked like a calculated insult.

At grass-roots level, Turkey's EU process was of no real concern during the campaign. Instead issues closer to home, such as high unemployment and poor housing, were in the forefront of people's minds. The moderate pro-Islamic AK Party promised a start to Turkey's EU entry talks and to create political stability, paving the way for an improvement of the economy.

Most compelling, an overall vision of a better future with Turkey as an EU member was repeatedly projected by the AK Party. The EU bid was also a fight for its legitimacy and survival as a political party. It gave the AK Party and its leader Erdoğan plenty of exposure. It also forged a growing network of political leaders abroad, which created a certain degree of protection against legal threats facing the AK Party and its leader. There was a real danger of the AK Party being banned even after being democratically elected. The State is the pillar and protector of Turkey's staunch secularism. If the AK Party did not tread very carefully it could easily be banned by the judiciary. It is a fairly frequent measure which political parties of Kurdish and religious affiliations have been faced with over the years. The AK Party's passionate drive for an EU accession appeared genuine. It was also a matter of enlightened self-interest.

Political Islam is not allowed according to the strictly secular state stipulated by the Constitution. The Islamic Welfare Party (*Refah Partisi*) was banned in 1998. The same fate occurred to its follower *Fazilet* in the summer of 2001, just over a year before the general election. The closure of Fazilet, in which the AK Party has its political roots, was condemned by the EU. It showed the need for political reforms in Turkey, stated the EU Presidency without really expecting a reversal of the courts' decision. No reversal occurred. Uncertainty about its future clouded the horizon for the AK Party and its leader throughout the election year and beyond.

Weak electoral competition

The weak coalition government slowly disintegrated as the election approached in the autumn of 2002. A far-reaching EU reform process had been successfully launched a year earlier, which had strong popular support. It was not enough to keep the Ecevit coalition government together. The economic crises kept overshadowing its EU accomplishments.

Foreign Minister Ismail Cem (of the Democratic Left Party), well known in the EU corridors of Brussels and very well liked and respected by his EU counterparts, was one of the cabinet ministers who left to form a new party. The attempt by the democratic political left to re-establish itself by founding new parties failed. They left made little impact during the campaign and on Election Day. Many Turks, whom I had met over the years, expressed their disappointment and frustration over the lack of a genuine social democratic movement with staying power in their country.

Despite being controversial, the election brought an end to decades of weak coalition governments. It also ended a long period of fragmented Turkish politics. The victory of the AK Party was expected as election day approached but their strong majority came as a huge surprise to most.

A coalition government had been predicted. The AK Party was the only untested major party in the running and yet was widely popular. The staunchly secular Republican People's Party (*Cumhurriyet Halk Partisi*; CHP), founded by Atatürk, was favoured by the domestic business sector. The two parties were expected to end up sharing power. Instead, the AK Party managed to secure a comfortable majority in Parliament by winning 34 per cent of the votes. The CHP returned to Parliament after three years out in the cold by receiving 19 per cent of the votes. The first single-party government in twenty years could be formed.

The AK Party gained almost two thirds of the 550 seats in Parliament. Proportionally, that is substantially higher than the 34 per cent of the votes that it received. The extremely high threshold (10 per cent) for political parties to get into Parliament worked in the pro-Islamic party's favour. This is somewhat paradoxical since the high barrier was not only introduced to discourage fragmentation of political parties into small units, it was also a way of keeping Islamists and Kurdish parties from gaining seats in Parliament.

Kurdish separatism and Islamism are traditionally viewed by the Turkish state and its military as major internal threats against the strict secular society. That the AK Party came from a lineage of religiously oriented political parties made its sudden dominance in Parliament and in power even more remarkable. Without a commanding aim to join the EU, its future as a party was likely to have been in serious jeopardy.

Among the EU ambassadors, predictions mainly centred on yet another coalition government coming to power. Apart from the AK Party, it was far from certain which other parties might be included.

Tancu Çiller, Turkey's first and so far only female prime minister and her conservative True Path Party (*Doğru Yol Partisi*; DYP) looked likely to make a return to national politics. Mrs Çiller gave a strikingly confident lunch briefing for the EU ambassadors shortly before the election. She had no doubts in her mind about a political comeback.

It was my first meeting with her and I was rather surprised. Tancu Çiller's time as a glamorous but controversial prime minister in the early 1990s attracted much international attention. She was then often described as someone who spoke better English than Turkish after twenty years as an economics professor on the east Coast of the US. Yet her cautiously-spoken English, often searching for words, contrasted with that perception. In the end, her True Path Party failed to be elected into Parliament, with less than a one per cent margin. The opportunity was lost to return as a coalition partner in the new government.

At a private party for around ten EU ambassadors, which my husband and I held in the amazing Cappadocian landscape of central Turkey, the dinner ended up being spent betting on the election outcome. The setting for the celebrations of our wedding anniversary was a small hotel, carved out from a volcanic rock, typical of the moon-landscaped Cappadocia. The Finnish ambassador Castrén, a wonderful old-fashioned gentleman, won the betting with almost faultless predictions. He claimed he could not see his own writing in the cave dining room, lit up by only a fireplace and candles, and was most surprised when it turned out that he had won. So were some of us other ambassadors who were more competitive and secretly deeply disappointed to have lost.

In discussions in diplomatic circles back in Ankara, the US embassy also turned out to have made strikingly accurate predictions of the upcoming elections. The Americans made no secret of their expectations. A convincing AK Party victory was viewed as the best option for the US. A war in Iraq appeared increasingly unavoidable and Turkish support of its NATO ally was expected. A new and strong party, like the AK, in search of international legitimacy, would be the safest bet. Time was to prove otherwise.

The left–right coalition partners in the Ecevit government were swept away from power, faced with a crushing defeat. 'They are put on history's garbage dump' was one harsh remark in a Turkish newspaper. The election defeat brought the seventy-eight-year-old Prime Minister Bülent Ecevit's forty-year-long political career to an end. A living monument to Turkish politics was gone. His party, the Democratic Left Party (*Demokrat Sol Partisi*; DSP), received only a humiliating one per cent of the votes. Neither of his two coalition partners in government managed to be re-elected into Parliament.

When I had moved to Ankara, I had looked forward to meeting the statesman Bülent Ecevit. He was well-known and highly regarded by many in Sweden for his poetry, journalism and political commitment to social democracy, inspired by the Nordic countries. My brief encounters with the elderly prime minister revealed a painfully frail man during his last couple of years in power. He was heading a cabinet consisting of three parties and thirty-five ministers, one of the world's largest, which hampered swift and critical decisions. The five-times prime minister increasingly lacked the strength and conviction to pursue the EU integration process.

This lack of strong commitment to the EU process, against a backdrop of economic crises, benefited the AK Party, which came across as a young, dynamic party with a highly result-driven EU policy. This is a rare occurrence in fragmented Turkish politics, where the personalities of political leaders are traditionally more important than policies. At the same time, the charismatic personality of Erdoğan could not be overlooked. He presented himself as fresh; as a break with the past. It was a strong pulling factor for the AK Party during the election even given the political controversy around him.

Joy and fear

Despite popular support and a strong performance in the election, many question marks surrounded the AK Party. At grass-roots level it was believed that Turkey had for the first time elected a party that truly represented the people rather than being the choice of the establishment. These sentiments differed sharply among many secular Turks. But there was common ground across the division between strongly secular forces and those wanting more freedom for Islam in society. There was a joint desire to ensure that Turkey obtained its rightful place in the EU. This vision was shared by the overwhelming majority, regardless of their background.

'This election means Turkey will become like Iran,' was one of the comments I heard while waiting for the election results to come in. It lingered in my mind years later. At first I thought it was a joke but soon realized it was not. There was a genuine fear of Islamists having gained power. Only then did I become fully aware of the intensity of feeling that the incoming ruling party aroused. The 1979 Khomeini Revolution across the Turkish border had left Turkey with enduring qualms. Suspicion and apprehension of what to expect next were widespread among staunchly secular Turks. Similar emotions emerged, during the embittered presidential elections five years later.

The AK Party's charismatic leader Tayyip Erdoğan, a devout Muslim who had been jailed for inciting religious hatred and who was banned for life from holding political office, was the undisputed winner. He was to spearhead Turkey's new, relentless EU bid.

Paving the way for an AK Party landslide victory

The success of the AK Party in the 2002 elections marked a turning point in Turkish politics. The majority of voters rejected what were perceived as old, corrupt and elitist political parties. There was an urge and desire for a radical change, on which the AK Party was able to capitalize. Being a newly established party with a young, captivating leader coming from a modest background emphasized this image. The party involved grass-roots support during the election campaign in an unprecedented way. Among the supporters, many women were helping out by knocking on doors, distributing election material.

It was a weak and crumbling three-party coalition government that entered into the election campaign in the summer of 2002. Intense speculation about the likely timing of the next election had started several months beforehand. The deteriorating health of Prime Minister Ecevit was continually being discussed. The divisions and fatigue among the ruling parties were obvious. Politics were on hold while leading personalities were positioning themselves among the established parties or choosing to branch out. The wide-ranging EU reform process, ambitiously launched in 2001, came to a gradual halt.

Unemployment, widespread corruption and general discontent with politicians paved the way for the AK Party, which promised a new, fresh start. Top priority was given to opening membership talks with the EU.

As the successful former mayor of Istanbul, Erdoğan was a well-known politician throughout Turkey. He was a crucial asset for his party, despite the legal and political controversies surrounding him. But his lack of experience of international politics was viewed with concern by several EU colleagues behind closed doors. I always found this lack a weak argument against Erdoğan's suitability as a future national leader. If you can successfully run a city twice the size of London and with a population that exceeds the size of many of the EU countries, you will also be able to learn the intricacies of foreign policy.

Remarkably few people speak any foreign languages in Ankara, including in political circles. The situation is different in cosmopolitan Istanbul. The language barrier was pretty solid, which limited interaction at social functions in the capital. It is very rare that Western ambassadors speak Turkish, with the British ambassador usually being an exception. This lack of a common language can restrict social life somewhat. Many social events in Ankara take place with those few Turks who speak any of the major European languages. They usually come from a privileged background of private schools in Turkey, studies abroad and frequent travel overseas. Many of those are staunchly secular and sceptical towards the AK Party. It is not surprising that their concerns made a certain impact on foreign envoys.

The AK Party had an image problem vis-à-vis the EU countries. It was largely unknown. Its democratic and secular credentials were untested. The majority of its top politicians spoke little or no foreign languages, precluding meetings without constant interpretation. These disadvantages were counteracted by an energetic briefing offensive made to each and every EU ambassador in town. I had two of the party's young founding members give an in-depth presentation in fluent English. They were dressed in dark suits, had no beards and were completely comfortable dealing with a female, including shaking hands. My first impressions were of professionalism and enthusiasm. The party's policy programme was surprisingly detailed for a brand-new party.

The AK Party had launched a two-track approach; wooing the voters while becoming acquainted with and introducing the new party to the EU ambassadors in Turkey. The party's energy and focus during the campaign were unrivalled among the political parties. It paid off on election day. Those who voted for the AK Party were mostly poor people in the rural areas. Yet even the results in Ankara, Istanbul and some Kurdish towns in the southeast were surprisingly good and beyond the expectations of the AK Party.

AK Party positions: Justice and development

It must be an almost unique situation, for a brand-new party to be elected into power fifteen months after its inception. The AK Party's quick ascent elicited awe in political circles abroad. Several politicians I met from EU member states visiting Turkey were fascinated. 'What is the magic trick?' they often asked. 'Listen to your voters,' was an answer often given by one of the AK Party's founding members, Reha Denemeç. He was a young, friendly parliamentarian from Ankara, in charge of research and development at the party headquarters. That included analysing public opinion based on frequent surveys carried out by the party.

It is no coincidence that the AK Party chooses to have an acronym meaning 'white' or 'clean' in Turkish. Corruption is a longstanding and endemic problem in Turkey. Few believe deep down that it will be stamped out in the foreseeable future. The AK Party's full name, the Justice and Development Party, was decided after sounding out what the key areas were for voters. Justice and development were most frequently mentioned in surveys carried out before the founding of the AK Party, hence the name.

This shows a liberating lack of apprehension of being accused of populism. Instead there was an obvious pride in naming the party purely based on people's concerns. I experienced this during my various meetings with the political leadership, which included more than ten deputy leaders. All were men. During some of those meetings, I could not help getting the impression that some of the elderly ones were unused to tête-à-tête appointments with a woman.

A similar situation occurred during my time as ambassador in Beirut. While I was having a luncheon meeting with the head of the foreign affairs committee in Parliament, who came from a prominent Shi'i Muslim family, he matter-of-factly stated that he had never met with a woman in a comparable situation before. In Turkey, where people initially tend to be more reserved and less spontaneous than in Lebanon, I never heard such an explicit comment. Still, I felt their unfamiliarity with the situation strongly. This was especially the case when travelling to distant parts of the country and meeting with local dignitaries, almost exclusively men.

An exception was in the small town of Hakkari near the Syrian border, which was unusual in having a female mayor. She came from a local, prominent family and was brimming with a vision for her town as a historic tourist destination for Christians and Muslims. However, she was unable to pursue this after losing power in the local elections in 2004.

Turkey is strikingly modern on the surface in the main cities, but extremely traditional beneath, even tribal in some poor, remote areas. No matter where I visited, Turkish hospitality was impeccable. Once it had been established during the initial small talk that I had a husband and children the atmosphere felt somewhat more relaxed. I might be a rare species of career woman from a remote European country, but I was also like most other women; a mother and a wife.

The AK Party is best described as a conservative, reform-oriented party. Family values are strong. Although similarities exist, it is reluctant to be compared to the Christian Democrats of Western Europe. That might change if the resistance of Christian Democrats in Germany to fully-fledged Turkish EU membership ever disappears. Any religious descriptions, such as the party being 'moderate Islam', are rejected. 'Is there such a thing as immoderate Islam?' Erdoğan often replied rhetorically when the question was brought up.

The party is frequently described by its own members as secular but with a Muslim identity. There is not a single reference to Islam in the AK Party's elaborate first election manifesto. A lesson was learnt from the Islamic Welfare Party, which was forced from power in 1997 after immense pressure from the secular establishment and the military.

The country's first Islamic prime minister, Erbakan, failed to replace what he believed to be Turkey's pathetic imitation of the West with worldwide Muslim solidarity. He was ousted from power in the first 'postmodern' coup in 1997. It changed the direction of the reformists within the Welfare Party. Erbakan was initially the political mentor of Erdoğan, but they fell out years before the AK Party was founded. A new openness to the modern world was adopted by the

AK Party. The EU entry bid became a cornerstone of its new foreign policy.

Apart from holding the EU bid as a top priority, few changes on foreign policy were expected. The new, major policy decisions on Iraq and Cyprus therefore came as huge surprises. In domestic policy, the attitude towards the IMF became more positive. Prime Minister Ecevit felt strongly ambivalent towards its presence in the country, at least initially. The incoming AK government viewed the IMF differently and saw the reforms as necessary. 'But we will not come as beggars,' underlined Erdoğan. Some of the IMF's programme was even identically worded in the AK Party manifesto. To combat the economic malaise, especially inflation, was a prime target and closely linked to Turkey's EU ambitions.

Relations with the secular establishment were another daunting challenge. Mutual lack of trust did not bode well for the future. Opponents viewed the AK Party and Erdoğan as closet Islamists. They feared that the enthusiasm for EU freedom reforms was merely a fig leaf from behind which secularism could be dismantled.

The AK Party's sensitive relationship with the powerful military was another delicate issue to tackle. Enormous domestic and international demands were piling up in front of the incoming government. The outcome was not easy to predict. If willpower were enough, though, the AK Party stood a fair chance of succeeding.

From political prisoner to prime minister: A personal profile of Tayyip Erdoğan

There is an ongoing 'Erdoğan experiment' in Turkish politics. Erdoğan is a devout Muslim in a highly secular society, a reformist in a region where democracy is scarce and a pragmatic pro-Westerner in a country with widespread anti-Americanism. His political ascent started almost a decade before the AK Party swept to power. When Erdoğan became Istanbul's first Islamist mayor in 1994, at the age of forty, he became a nationally known politician. He has remained in the headlines ever since.

His controversial imprisonment in 1999 only enhanced his standing among his admirers. It raised doubts even within secular circles. Turkey's apparent lack of freedom of expression was questioned. And Erdoğan's five months behind bars changed him. Ever since, he has viewed himself as a victim of human rights abuses. During my many meetings with Erdoğan he often came back to this. There was deep disappointment, even traces of bitterness, over the lack of action from Europe following his conviction. His reaction is understandable. He was imprisoned for quoting the Turkish ideologue and nationalist, Ziya Gökalp, at an election rally: 'Minarets are our bayonets, Domes are our helmets, Mosques are our barracks, Believers are our soldiers.' Paradoxically, the identical quotation can be found in government textbooks in state schools across the country.

A few months after the landslide election, Erdoğan was still waiting for his lifelong ban on holding political office to be lifted. He could not yet move into the prime minister's office in the crowded, central part of Ankara. The AK Party heavyweight Abdullah Gül was the obvious candidate to temporarily hold the post of prime minister. In the meantime Erdoğan had his base in the rented party headquarters in a quiet and undistinguished part of the capital.

Erdoğan's office was fairly large, but bland and impersonal. There was no clutter and few pictures except for the customary large image of Atatürk. This is in every single government office and public place in Ankara. The only decorations were a few framed copies of French impressionists on the walls. A traditional oversized corner room to emphasize the occupier's importance was hardly needed.

Erdoğan's charisma was definitely evident. His athletic, towering body and commanding voice leave a strong impression as he greets you in English before switching back to Turkish. His natural authority and seriousness are striking. So is his self-control, which makes him difficult to fathom. His lengthy reasoning is rarely interrupted by any of the many senior advisers surrounding him. As I was once leaving the office of Erdoğan's headquarters in his private elevator, I found that the inner peace he radiates left the strongest impression. Even his fiercest political opponents must envy him that.

Recep Tayyip Erdoğan's first-hand experience of human rights violations seems to have cemented his conviction to push through EU reforms. Growing up in a poor area of Istanbul did not hold him back from gaining a university degree. A successful business career in the food industry followed before he entered full-time politics. More than ten years as a semi-professional soccer player have left him with much-needed stamina. He will certainly need it during the years ahead in the EU accession process. Negotiations at home and in Brussels are likely to be his toughest struggles yet.

Erdoğan's strongest opponents still view him as a wolf in sheep's clothing. They fear the EU human rights reforms are merely a fig leaf, and that secularism will be gradually removed, political Islam will resurface under a human rights banner and the EU membership bid be abandoned as soon as it is no longer needed.

On the other hand, it could well turn out that in Erdoğan Turkey has a leader who, together with Abdullah Gül, will complete Atatürk's half-finished revolution of Westernization and modernization by achieving a Turkish EU membership. Erdoğan looks likely to remain a key player in Turkish politics for decades to come. It will be necessary for EU countries and others to learn to understand him and his party. His quick ascent in Turkish politics was not enough to take him to the presidency in the summer of 2007 but next time around, when the president for the first time will be elected by popular vote, he might well be rewarded with the highest office.

From election victory to the EU

It was the morning after the 2002 election. The Swedish foreign minister, Anna Lindh, who had a passionate interest in Turkey, rang. She was on her way to Mexico together with the Swedish king and queen but was keen to discuss the election. I was in the unusual and challenging situation of having a cabinet minister whose knowledge about my host country far exceeded that of most diplomats. She was excited about the new political situation in Turkey and its prospects for making progress on democracy and human rights. Her position as a Social Democrat while the new government was Conservative was secondary to the possibilities which now opened up.

For several years, the Swedish government was one of the most vocal critics of Turkey's serious violations of human rights within the EU and at the United Nations. At the EU summit in Helsinki in 1999, Sweden was one of the last EU member states to agree to grant Turkey EU candidate status. This highly sceptical outlook on Turkey becoming a future EU partner began to alter, not only in Sweden.

New possibilities emerged as the Turkish political landscape had suddenly changed. After the election there was a sense of a fresh start for Turkey's four decades-long EU membership ambitions.

The first post-election meeting between Erdoğan and the EU

Only a few days after the election, a dinner meeting was held between Tayyip Erdoğan and the EU ambassadors in Ankara. With Denmark holding the rotating EU presidency at the time, the dinner was hosted at the Danish ambassador Christian Hoppe's ultra-modern residence, a stone's throw away from the presidential mansion. Turkey's passionate race to get a green light to start EU talks had begun. This took off several weeks before the new government had even been formed.

It was the first day of *Ramadan*, or *Ramazan* in Turkish, Islam's holy month of fasting. It was significant that the top leaders of the AK Party, such as Erdoğan and Gül, chose to spend the first evening of breaking the fast at an EU meeting. It illustrated the importance attached to the EU process by the incoming government. Maybe it even reduced some of the anxiety within Turkey's strongly secular society about their new political leaders' religiousness and their willingness to keep it exclusively private.

Erdoğan gave the EU ambassadors a number of concrete commitments. His reformist zeal was obvious. The strongest emphasis was put on a new policy of 'zero tolerance against torture'. A revision on certain human rights in the Constitution was also among the commitments. Erdoğan argued strongly for the EU to give Turkey a starting date for accession talks at the upcoming EU summit in Copenhagen the following month.

Among the arguments put forward by Erdoğan illustrating Turkey's strength was that a one-party government would speed up the EU process. There was huge support in Turkey for membership. Its strategic position, including 'its strong door vis-à-vis the Middle East' was also given as an example.

The Kurdish issue was still highly sensitive, if not taboo, in Turkish society. All inhabitants were regarded as Turks; a definition along ethnic lines was unacceptable. When I brought up the importance that my government attached to human rights and the concern it felt regarding the Kurdish issue, there was a surprisingly dismissive reply from Erdoğan. Human rights apply to all Turks, not only parts of the population. These problems had already been solved by the reforms adopted a few months previously, he stated. Given the charged atmosphere and his political ban at the time it was probably the only thing he could say. It was still worthwhile, I felt, to make a point. Without further reforms for the Kurds the Turkish EU process would not move forward much. When I mentioned the super sensitive 'K-word' one could have heard a pin drop in the elegant dining room of the Danish ambassador.

The same day, in a comment on how to solve the Cyprus question, Erdoğan had mentioned the Belgian model of cohabitation. That resulted in fierce condemnation in the Turkish media, which accused him of being a traitor. There was no such thing as a honeymoon for the victorious AK Party leader.

Business sector rallied behind EU bid

The local business community was fully behind the AK Party's campaign leading up to the EU summit in 2002. Although initially supportive of the Republican People's Party (CHP), pragmatism prevailed. As the AK Party was getting ready to take over power, the business sector rallied behind it in the EU campaign.

The influential Turkish industrialists' group, *Tüsiad*, launched a huge media campaign abroad. Full-page ads in a British newspaper showed Tony Blair, a strong supporter of Turkish EU membership, with the caption 'The only way to have a friend is to be one'. In Austria, known for its scepticism towards the Turkish EU bid, the message to Chancellor Wolfgang Schüssel was 'Don't pull up the plant to see if it's growing'. The message to all EU capitals was that Turkey now was a stable, young, dynamic and culturally rich country ready to make a real contribution to European peace and prosperity. The key message was 'Don't miss the historic opportunity in Copenhagen to open the way for Turkey'.

Whistle-stop tour to EU capitals

Recep Tayyip Erdoğan intended to make a whistle-stop tour to meet all political leaders in the EU capitals – fifteen at the time – in an attempt to secure a starting date for accession talks. His plans caused consternation, with some capitals not knowing how to receive him. He was the obvious winner of the election but not prime minister-designate. Also, he was still banned from holding public office. In the end, he was received by prime ministers in the EU member states. Later, they were to become his counterparts.

The then Swedish prime minister Göran Persson was one of the first to agree to receive him. At their meeting Erdoğan emphasized political will as the key to change. As mayor of Istanbul he had ended corruption in one month and achieved a ten-fold increase in income tax. The importance of his support from the main opposition party and 80 per cent of the population was also highlighted. Although Erdoğan had little experience of high-level foreign policy talks, it was his confidence and zeal which left the strongest impressions as he was departing Stockholm after less than twenty-four hours. It was a typical dark November day. He arrived and left in darkness and could hardly have seen anything apart from meeting rooms during his first visit to Sweden. It was still *Ramazan*. The fruit baskets on the conference table were left untouched by Erdoğan.

If hesitation prevailed within the EU towards Turkey's EU bid, the message from the other side of the Atlantic was clear. The US administration gave unreserved and active support for Turkey to be offered a starting date for EU membership negotiations. President Bush and Secretary of State Colin Powell lobbied intensively as the EU summit approached.

In spite of all efforts, it was still not enough. At the 2002 Copenhagen summit the EU leaders decided not to set a date for Turkish accession talks. But it was half a victory. The EU committed itself to reviewing the situation at the EU summit two years later, in Brussels in December 2004. Accession negotiations with Turkey would start without delay if the political demands on human rights and democracy (the so-called Copenhagen Criteria) were met.

An initially angry and disappointed reaction from the new Turkish government quickly subsided. It was replaced by a certain degree of satisfaction, a reaction encouraged by the EU. If not a milestone, it was still a major breakthrough in EU–Turkish relations.

Relentless reforms on human rights and democracy were launched during the next two years. An often unanimous Parliament pushed through one reform package after another. There were very frequent meetings between Turkish government officials and the EU embassies in Ankara. To serve as a diplomat in Turkey during that time was extraordinary and exciting. It was like going back to a traditional diplomacy when embassy dispatches were one of the very few channels of information to the Foreign Office back home.

Knowledge of the changing face of Turkey was limited. While there was close contact between the EU capitals, EU governments had few continuous contacts with their political counterparts in Ankara. There were several reasons for this. The language barrier and, initially, the lack of personal contacts limited exchange or interaction. Western media were scarce in Ankara. On the other hand, many foreign journalists lived and worked in Istanbul. Although only an hour away by air, or five hours' drive on a modern highway, it often felt a world apart.

Leadership change after only three months

Abdullah Gül stepped down quietly as prime minister only three months after taking up office. Rumours claiming he would not step aside voluntarily turned out to be completely unfounded. It showed a lack of understanding of the party hierarchy. It was a smooth leadership transition. Interestingly, there were no significant hints of rivalry or resentment despite the shift taking place between the party's two strong men and natural leaders. Their only potential rival at the time, Mr Bülent Arinç, had swiftly and successfully earmarked for himself the position of Speaker of Parliament.

Erdoğan's political ban was lifted. In a by-election he secured more than 90 per cent of the votes. It took place in his wife Emine's home town of Siirt in the southeast in March 2003, four months after the general election. Siirt is a small town near the Syrian and Iraqi borders.

On a visit there, I stayed as one of the few guests in the town's only hotel, owned by a former politician. I saw no women out on the streets in the evening. School children on the streets turned around pointing and waving at me. I felt as though I was the first blond and blue-eyed person to visit there. Arabic was known by many. As usual, the hospitality was exceptional. The most wonderful food was offered; a mixture of Turkish, eastern Mediterranean, Kurdish and Arabic cuisine.

Gül was in many ways the opposite of his party leader. Gül had long experience of national and international politics, both in Parliament and from the Council of Europe. As the new foreign minister, starting in spring 2003, his main task was to develop the EU process at home and in Brussels. Erdoğan kept a high international profile as the driving force behind Turkey's EU process. He travelled abroad almost non-stop.

Gül's gentle personality, in-depth knowledge and softly-spoken approach won over many a critic. One young and chic Turkish woman from Istanbul whom I met described Gül affectionately as Turkey's George Clooney, while stressing that she did not vote for the AK Party.

After the brutal murder in Stockholm of Foreign Minister Anna Lindh in 2003, sometimes described as an adversary or even enemy of Turkey, Gül was one of the first to call me. Without remembering exactly what he said, I recall that his condolences went beyond the usual conventional phrases. He shared the sentiment of personal and professional loss of one of the most vocal supporters within the EU of Turkey's reform process.

Adultery threatened progress

A frenzy of new legislations and reforms were introduced. One reform package after another was passed in Parliament, mostly with the support of the only opposition party. Only occasionally was new legislation vetoed by President Ahmet Necdet Sezer, a former high court judge. The business sector was supportive and civil society flourishing. Torture in prisons became less prevalent. Freedom of expression was enhanced. Women's rights within marriage were strengthened and harsher punishment introduced for 'honour crimes'.

There were only rare occasions when the government came near to stumbling. One such occasion occurred in spring 2004. The impressive and rapid process of reform was threatened by a proposal pushed forward by the prime minister. Erdoğan's personal desire to have adultery criminalized sent shivers through the European capitals. Secular society in Turkey felt their worst fears of an Islamic government with *sharia* law leanings were being realised. There was a sense of shock.

I had received a leather-bound Qur'an as a Christmas gift from a Turkish trade union leader only a few months earlier. I kept it on my bedside table, reading it at night without ever finding any justification to criminalize adultery.

The reasoning behind Erdoğan's proposal, which he explained to me at a dinner in Istanbul, was intriguing and unexpected. He viewed it as a way of protecting abandoned wives, left without alimony and child support, who had husbands living with another woman. Rumours were rife that it was originally an idea conceived by either Emine Erdoğan, the wife of the prime minister, or one of the leading female AK Party members of parliament, a lawyer. These seemed, though, more based on guess work than on fact. After immense pressure from all quarters, including Erdoğan's own inner circle of advisers, he did change his mind. The proposal was dropped and the reform process was back on track.

A historic 'yes' to Turkish accession talks

There was a diplomatic frenzy in December 2004 as the grand finale of Turkey's EU bid was approaching. 'We have historic hours in front of us,' said a hopeful but tough-talking Erdoğan in a lunch meeting with EU ambassadors just two days before the EU summit in Brussels.

The meeting was hosted in his modern official residence in Ankara, up the hill in the Çankaya district, overlooking the city.

On becoming prime minister, he chose to live in an unassuming home in a modest part of Ankara rather than move into the elegant, official mansion. This was a way to remain close to his electorate. The official residence was only used for hosting meetings such as the one with the EU ambassadors. On the Turkish side, Erdoğan was accompanied by around twenty political and diplomatic advisors. All in all, we were around fifty people, all sitting at one enormously long table. I was sitting almost opposite Erdoğan in the centre and next to the Dutch ambassador Sjoerd Gosses, who held the EU Presidency. The seating depended on how long one had served in the country. So after three and a half years in Ankara I was seated close to the host as guest of honour.

The most difficult issue to handle would be if the EU decided on open-ended negotiations, underlined Erdoğan. To have formulations stating that the end result was not guaranteed would be 'humiliating and dreadful'. He predicted no major problems at the summit regarding Cyprus since it was not part of the EU's Copenhagen Criteria. Turkey had already done all it possibly could. 'Believe me, we will not beg the EU. We are already together in NATO, the Council of Europe, OSCE (Organisation for Security and Cooperation in Europe) and other organizations; why is it so difficult to digest Turkey this time around?' Erdoğan asked rhetorically.

Putting an end to the use of systematic torture and enhancing freedom and rights have been the most successful elements so far during the intensive reform process. That was Erdoğan's answer when I asked him to single out the government's major achievements in the EU process since coming to power. 'No question is insurmountable. If we are only allowed to start negotiations we will solve the rest along the way,' said a confident Erdoğan.

It was obvious that there was no concrete 'Plan B' in case the EU would not give Turkey a starting date for negotiations. 'It would not be the end; reforms will continue but no longer called Copenhagen but Ankara criteria,' said the prime minister. 'Regardless of what decision the EU will make, we don't expect manna from heaven,' Erdoğan declared.

After the meeting he took me aside to thank Sweden for its support. Sweden had come full circle in a period of only a few years; from being one of the most ardent critics of the Turkish EU bid to being among its strongest supporters for full membership at the end of the process.

As Turkey was transforming itself and membership negotiations becoming increasingly likely, anti-Turkish sentiments were emerging within the EU. Until then these had seldom been raised in Ankara. But as Turkey's drive for EU integration picked up pace, so did the scepticism and opposition to Turkey becoming a future full member of 'the Club'.

The domestic political climate cooled significantly before the EU summit in December 2004. 'Turkey risks ending up as Europe's mistress and nothing else,' warned the opposition leader Deniz Baykal. His CHP Party feared that the price for a starting date for negotiations would be too high. Concessions on Cyprus were the main sticking point.

The government went to Brussels with strong support among the people. More than 70 per cent of the population supported future EU membership. No other EU country or candidate country had that solid support for the organization. In the Kurdish area in the southeast, as many as 90 per cent were pro-EU.

Difficult political debates preceded the December 2004 EU summit. It became a political baptism of fire for the Dutch EU Presidency. The Cyprus position and whether negotiations would automatically lead to membership turned out to be the two most complex issues. When the Turkish delegation threatened to walk out, an eleventh-hour decision was made. No resolution was found to the highly contentious Cyprus issue which was again put on hold. In addition, Turkey had to accept that there were no guarantees being given for membership.

The Dutch Presidency had not counted on the Turkish delegation initially being so headstrong. This included the Dutch foreign minister Bernard Bot, who was a former ambassador to Turkey. 'Turkey has accepted the EU's extended hand and together we have made history, although the agreement will only take shape in the future,' declared a relieved Dutch Prime Minister Balkenendes on 17 December 2004.

Prime Minister Erdoğan returned to a hero's welcome in Ankara. His display of tough-talking and brinkmanship was praised. The mass-circulation *Hürriyet*, traditionally highly critical of the AK government, trumpeted 'We did it!' Another daily newspaper, *Zaman*, had 'A New Europe, a New Turkey' as its headline. Huge banners congratulating the prime minister hung across the main boulevard in Ankara, Atatürk Bulvari, which runs through the city.

An invitation from local politicians to join in formally greeting Erdoğan upon his return to the capital reached me only a couple of hours before his arrival. I was curious and tempted to go but decided against it. It could be construed as too much of party politics for me to participate as a foreign ambassador. My fourteen-year-old daughter went with some friends to have a look at the downtown celebrations, only a few blocks away from our residence in the leafy Kavaklidere district.

Was the historic breakthrough for Turkey at the EU summits in Copenhagen in 2002 and Brussels two years later merely due to a combination of favourable circumstances? Was pure luck with timing one of them? Could the AK Party government simply reap the fruit of decades of effort by its predecessors?

Domestic situation changed for the better

Domestically, the capture of the terrorist group PKK leader Öcalan in 1999 was followed by years of relative calm. The conflict between the army and the terrorist group subsided. The violent separatist struggle in the Kurdish southeast was replaced by a truce for the first time in more than fifteen years. Widespread human rights violations became much less frequent and emergency rule was lifted. Some cultural rights were granted to the Kurds. The Kurdish problem was far from solved but sufficiently dealt with. It paved the way for the EU to grant Turkey a starting date for negotiations.

This was not only down to the single issue of the Kurds. The single-party government had an unprecedented focus on achieving a breakthrough in Turkey's EU process. A new momentum was created. The personal experiences of human rights abuses among its top leadership only seemed to strengthen the government's commitment to reforms. 'The Turkish people deserve these reforms,' Erdoğan said often in meetings with the EU ambassadors in Ankara. He viewed himself, probably correctly, as the first grass-roots leader of the country. Only Bülent Ecevit in the 1970s could match that image. He had broken the tradition of elitist politicians representing the people. His top priority was to transform Turkey in order to improve the life of the ordinary citizen. When Mr Ecevit passed away in Ankara, aged eighty-one, in November 2006, after a six-month coma, his funeral ceremony attracted huge crowds.

The threat to the very existence of the AK Party was another incentive to succeed with the EU criteria. Its secular credentials were constantly questioned. It lacked full legitimacy in the eyes of the Turkish establishment. The democratization of the country effectively became a safeguard to the future of the AK Party itself.

The government managed to establish good working relations with the military and its then chief-of-staff, General Hilmi Özkök, a man with whom I always found it a delight to have discussions. He was open, razor-sharp and very friendly. There appeared to be an attitude between Prime Minister Erdoğan and General Özkök of giving each other the benefit of the doubt. Against all odds, the relationship seemed, at least initially, surprisingly comfortable and effective. A *modus vivendi* prevailed during the first few years. The influence of the military's political role was reduced as part of the reform process, though many would argue that its *de facto* influence is unchanged. Importantly, without the military's consent to step back from its crucial role in political decision-making, the reform process would have suffered substantially. Few would have anticipated the cold war that suddenly erupted between the AK government and the military in 2007 over the choice of the next president.

Sweeping political and economic reforms, backed up by the EU and the IMF, created a new economic environment. Interest rates and inflation were drastically reduced. For the first time since 1970 inflation was below 10 per cent and the interest rate down from 70 to 13 per cent. Political stability put an end to the devastating economic crisis which had paralyzed the country at the beginning of the new millennium.

I was first introduced to Ali Babacan, a successful businessman in his mid-thirties, by the head of the IMF in Turkey. We were outside a Chinese restaurant in Ankara during a stiflingly hot evening in July 2002. There were four months left until the general election. Ali Babacan had become Minister of the Economy, just as the head of the IMF had predicted months earlier. The softly-spoken and exceptionally bright Babacan held an unfaltering belief in the AK Party's ability to turn the economy around. He was proven right, at least during the first few years. Only time will tell if the U-turn of the Turkish economy is durable or not.

Favourable domestic developments were obviously far from the only explanations for the historic EU decision to grant Turkey a starting date for accession talks. External factors, beyond the control of the EU and Turkey, also contributed.

The 9/11 terror attacks in the US led to an enhanced geopolitical role for Turkey. Its marginalization following the end of the cold war was over. Turkey was no longer needed as a barrier against communism. Instead, as a secular yet Muslim country and loyal NATO ally it made the perfect partner in the US-led war against terror following the attacks in New York and Washington. Turkey's expertise and military contributions in fighting terrorism in Afghanistan underlined its new, enhanced role.

The war in Iraq clouded and complicated public perception of Turkey's new-found role. This was particularly the case after the startlingly unexpected refusal to allow the US to enter Iraq through Turkey. Despite the rift which followed in US–Turkish relations, the Bush administration was unwavering in its support of Turkey's EU ambitions.

Turkey's geopolitical role became less vital than first envisaged after the 9/11 attacks. Instead Turkey took on a different, yet prominent role. It became an important proof that democracy and modernization are compatible in a country with a predominantly Muslim population.

It also became increasingly important to prove that the EU was not a 'Christian Club'. Otherwise, it was feared, there would be increased alienation among Muslims living in Europe. Allowing Turkey to start membership negotiations was an indicator of the EU's openness. Being the first, and so far only, EU candidate country with a predominantly Muslim population, Turkey was a test of the EU's multiculturalism.

Positive domestic developments paved the way for an end to Turkey's forty-year wait to commence membership talks. The terrorist attacks in the US in 2001, Madrid in spring 2004 and London in summer 2005, inspired by fundamentalist Muslims, increased anxiety about a clash between civilizations. This concern over a Western–Muslim fault line facilitated Turkey's EU bid.

EU optimism benefitted Turkey

The largest EU expansion ever, increasing it from fifteen to twenty-five countries and 500 million people in spring 2004, created an aura of success and strength. Internal, upbeat visions of the EU's own bright future contributed greatly to the positive decision towards Turkey. European integration and economic reforms seemed irreversible.

At a meeting in the Baltic capital Tallinn on the eve of the enlargement in May 2004, I talked to a young, female member of the Estonian Parliament. She recalled how her mother had cried from happiness as American military planes had flown over the tiny Baltic state when it joined NATO only a few weeks earlier. The old woman never thought she would live to see that as well as the imminent EU membership. Feelings of joy ran high in the country, which had regained its independence only thirteen years earlier.

There were few, if any, warning signs of looming enlargement fatigue. An unprecedented momentum existed. The EU looked as though it were heading towards becoming a world democratic power. In this period of glowing optimism, Turkey received support from all the key political EU leaders at the time: Tony Blair, always a robust supporter of Turkey's EU bid, German Chancellor Gerhard Schröder, French President Jacques Chirac (albeit without much support from his people or his own UMP party) and Italy's Silvio Berlusconi as well as his future successor Romano Prodi, who was the president of the EU Commission at the time.

History in the making

The historic decision reached at the 2004 EU summit illustrated the joint power of a pro-reform Turkish government and the EU as a positive catalyst in the process. The AK government would have struggled endlessly with its legitimacy at home and abroad without the EU track to follow. Furthermore, the deep reluctance among the Turkish establishment about the rapid speed of reforms could have become insurmountable for the government without the carrot that the EU offered.

It was a triumph for the EU's enlargement and 'soft power' foreign policy. It was also a victory for Turkey's ability to transform itself in only a few years through a silent revolution. This 'golden period' is frequently a unrecognized success story for the EU as well as Turkey but the final outcome is far from certain.

FIVE

From Human Rights Deficit to Progress

Dramatic developments in Diyarbakir

We were at a crowded State Security Court in Diyarbakir, a regional centre in the Kurdish-dominated southeast in early spring 2002. The distinguished Kurdish author Mehmed Uzun from Turkey, who came to Sweden as a political refugee in the late 1970s, was on trial. Here was an EU citizen who had fled his country, which now wanted to imprison him. While Uzun fought for freedom of speech and the right to one's mother tongue – the forbidden Kurdish language – the prosecutor saw it differently. He demanded a conviction for propagating separatism. It looked as though the author had become a pawn between Turkish pro-EU reformists and nationalists at a time when Turkey's EU reforms had started to take off like never before.

There were broad-based international protests against the prosecution from across Europe by writers' and translators' organizations. In addition, a committee of Swedish writers and lawyers, among them a former prosecutor at the Hague-based International Court of Justice and members of the prestigious, more-than-two-hundred-year-old Swedish Royal Academy, had been formed to support Uzun. The committee believed that the persecution of Uzun had intensified because of his position as the most widely read Kurdish-language writer, whose books (translated into many different languages, including Turkish) had met with wide acclaim all over Turkey. The committee accompanied Mehmed Uzun to the trial in Diyarbakir. The instruction from Foreign Minister Anna Lindh to the embassy in Ankara was straightforward: 'Diplomat presence at the trial goes without saying', which brought me on the same Turkish Airline plane to Diyarbakir as the defendant, a journey of more than 1,000 kilometres southeast of Ankara. The city, on the banks of the Tigris River, had sights and sounds creating an Oriental feel.

The trial was held in a stark, modern cement-block building near the centre of town, just outside the famous city walls, which date from early Byzantine times. Security was extremely tight. The corridor was packed with people attending various trials at the court, almost exclusively men. Every visitor's identity was checked. The atmosphere was thick with fear. In Mehmed Uzun's long statement of defence, which he read out himself, separatism was dismissed as something foolish and dangerous, while he defended the rights of Kurds to have their own language and culture. After less than an hour the trial was over and Mehmed Uzun acquitted due to lack of evidence. The third prosecution in only a couple of years had failed to convict him or his publisher. Despite enormous relief, the psychological toll taken was obvious.

Less than two years later Mehmed Uzun would be back in the same building, but in a completely different situation. The transformation of Turkey would bring about changes impossible to imagine as we stepped out of the State Security Court into the spring sunshine on 19 April 2002.

Fast forward to November 2003. In the same municipality building which housed the State Security Court, an international Kurdish writers' conference was being held in the town assembly hall. Mehmed Uzun was reading aloud from his latest novel *Light as*

Love, Dark as Death to a captivated audience of five hundred people. It was a tragic love story and a quiet but raw emotional account of confrontations between love and death, oppression and liberty – a tale of longing, violence and reconciliation. The same novel had been confiscated and led to another prosecution in Istanbul a couple of years earlier, in spring 2001.

Here Mehmed Uzun was at the centre of attention, back in his childhood neighbourhood participating in the first Kurdish writers' conference of its kind in the region. He was able to read publicly in his mother tongue, no longer forbidden after eighty years, from a book that had been confiscated only a few years earlier. All this was unfolding in the same building complex where he had stood trial only eighteen months ago. I could not but stop and reflect on seeing history in the making while attending the conference together with a Swedish parliamentarian human rights delegation, on a trip around Turkey.

Momentous progress had been achieved in only a few years' time. The Anti-Terror Law was amended and its Article 8, which was the basis for one of the prosecutor's cases against Uzun, was revoked by Parliament in July 2003. The State Security Courts were abolished through an amendment of the Penal Code by Parliament in June 2004. The state of emergency was able to be lifted in Diyarbakir after fifteen years. The Constitution was changed, lifting the ban on the use of the Kurdish language. State TV and radio began broadcasts in Kurdish and three other minority languages, although still with considerable restrictions. The wide availability of satellite dishes across the country already gave full access to foreign broadcasts, including several Kurdish-language private channels.

Sweden, which opened the world's first Kurdish library in the late 1990s in Stockholm, financed the publication of children's fairy-tale books in Kurdish in 2003. There was some apprehension as to whether this would result in negative reactions. The books were distributed to young children in and around Diyarbakir. The initiative received only positive responses.

Turkey had embraced a process of far-reaching constitutional and legislative reforms. Substantive steps towards European standards were being made in the human rights field. Turkey's EU candidature was rapidly starting to show that it was a robust catalyst for change. But the question remained as to what extent the reforms would be applied in practice and if they were sustainable. The next few years would be decisive.

Freedom of expression

Mehmed Uzun, who passed away, aged 53, in 2007 after a long illness, was far from being the only one to have faced legal harassment. Freedoms of expression, speech and the press are guaranteed in the Constitution. There is an active and lively debate in the media and in academic life on all aspects of government policies and on democracy and human rights, especially relating to Turkey's EU membership process. However, limitations restricting freedoms continue in some areas. To publicly criticize the State or Government can still not be done by individuals without some fear of reprisals. Sometimes there is self-censorship on sensitive issues such as the Armenian or Kurdish issues or the role of the military.

Dozens of writers, journalists and political figures have been brought to court every year in recent times by prosecutors, but their cases were often dismissed in the end by judges. Cartoonists are not excluded from recourse to legal action. It was, though, surprising and disappointing that Prime Minister Erdoğan was among those bringing charges against cartoonists in 2005, considering his own experience of imprisonment in 1998 on what appeared to be a violation of his freedom of expression.

The need for a changed mentality, a new way of thinking, became increasingly obvious in order to achieve a successful implementation of the many legislative reforms. With as much as a third of the

Constitution revised as part of the reforms, the need for further training was evident. The entire judiciary was targeted. The Turkish Ministry of Justice translated the jurisprudence of the European Court of Human Rights into Turkish with the aim of influencing the decision-making by the judiciary itself. More than 1,500 judges and prosecutors participated in seminars in EU countries such as Britain and Sweden, upon an initiative by the Turkish government in early 2003.

The Armenian issue

The Armenian issue is an example of a taboo which has been recently broken. It remains highly sensitive, a fact which many high-profile Turkish writers are aware of, having been prosecuted and some convicted for mentioning the 'Armenian genocide' of the early twentieth century. Allegations of a genocide of Armenians almost a century ago cause recurrent political storms in Turkey and have affected its EU bid. Although the issue itself is not part of the EU's Copenhagen Criteria it is increasingly viewed as an indicator of Turkey's progress on freedom of speech and expression. Thus, it is indirectly becoming a part of the accession negotiations.

Armenians claim that up to 1.5 million people died in massacres and forced mass deportations during the end of the Ottoman Empire. Turkey, on the other hand, says that famine, disease and widespread conflicts caused large numbers of people to perish, on both sides. It believes the controversial issue should be left to historians.

In a country where national pride is so important and sensitivity is high to criticism from abroad, the Armenian issue is not only affecting the EU process but also troubling some bilateral relations. Among them are those with France, Canada and Switzerland, and most recently the US, where a US congressional committee passed a resolution in autumn 2007 recognizing the mass killings of Armenians as genocide. Strong opposition by President Bush was not enough to stop the resolution from being passed (and with a larger majority than predicted) but it was later shelved after massive Turkish protests and faltering US–Turkish relations.

When the French National Assembly voted in late 2000 to recognize the killings of Armenians in 1915 as genocide, it had serious implications on French–Turkish political and economic relations. Another vote by the Assembly in Paris in October 2006, making it illegal to deny the genocide, put further strain on relations. It is now up to the French Senate to stop this bill, which is creating an unfortunate setback to freedom of expression.

The question remains deeply divisive. Turkish best-selling novelist Orhan Pamuk was prosecuted after saying in an interview with the Swiss newspaper *Tages Anzeiger* that '30,000 Kurds and one million Armenians were killed on these lands and almost nobody but me dares to talk about it'. He received death threats. His books were burnt on a bonfire in a town in southern Anatolia, which attracted international attention. Until then the small town near the Syrian border was only known outside Turkey to keen bird-watchers. The criminal charges against Pamuk for 'insulting Turkish identity' were dropped in January 2006, a move welcomed by the EU. Orhan Pamuk was the first Turk to be awarded a Nobel prize, but his accomplishment in 2006 was partly overshadowed by resentful reactions from some among the Turkish establishment who fiercely objected to his comments on the Armenian issue.

The most prominent Armenian voice in Turkey was the journalist Hrant Dink, who was convicted on similar charges in October 2005. He was a frequent target of nationalist anger for his outspoken position on the Armenian issue. Dink, fifty-three, who was raised in an orphanage in Istanbul, was murdered in broad daylight outside his office in Istanbul in January 2007. Judging from the widespread outpouring of grief and condemnation and the huge attendance at Hrant Dink's funeral in his home town, his death could catalyze a reconciliation process in Turkey. He will be remembered as a symbol of the importance of enshrining free speech, which vocal supporters of the perpetrators never will be able to overshadow.

A conference on 'Ottoman Armenians during the Collapse of the Empire: Scientific Responsibilities and Issues of Democracy' was initially meant to be held in spring 2005 at a university in Istanbul. The conference had to be postponed after criticism in Parliament by the Minister of Justice, and an administrative court's decision in Istanbul prevented it from taking place at the Bosporus University. Four months later, at another venue, Istanbul Bilgi University, the conference would be held with the support of Prime Minister Erdoğan. It illustrated that gradually progress is being made on a previously taboo question. However, it also showed the need for strong political leadership to make this happen.

Torture

During travels across the country, I started to meet with the heads of police in many of the towns that I visited. Initially I had not intended to include them, I must confess, when I requested various meetings with local officials such as the powerful governors, appointed by the government and employed by the Ministry of the Interior, and the elected mayors. But while visiting Mersin, an attractive harbour town on the Mediterranean coast, I was advised to pay a courtesy call on the police chief, who was highly regarded in the local community. He spoke fluent French and it was a rare and enjoyable occasion not to have to speak through a translator. That was almost always the case while meeting public officials or local politicians in different parts of Turkey, whether they were young or old. Some of them had been on English language courses abroad but lacked practice, therefore preferring to speak Turkish through a translator. The first police chief that I met with in Mersin in summer 2003 was so knowledgeable and hospitable that from then on I always tried to get an appointment with his counterparts in various towns that I visited. It was also an important opportunity to discuss one of the most difficult questions in the EU reform process: torture. Some police chiefs were visibly uncomfortable and discussed the problems of torture awkwardly. Their reactions were quite understandable. It was, though, a telling sign of the rapidly changing Turkey that they had to, or were willing to, receive me, an EU member state ambassador, to discuss the human rights situation. I am convinced that had it been attempted only a few years earlier, a request for a meeting would have been met with stony silence.

The Constitution explicitly prohibits torture and ill-treatment. 'No one shall be subjected to torture or ill-treatment; no one shall be subjected to penalty or treatment incompatible with human dignity.'[1] Nevertheless, it was a systemic and widespread problem in Turkey for decades. The first legal cases against torturers go back as early as the 1960s but without having led to any convictions during several decades.

Lately, different governments in Ankara had acknowledged that the practice of torture and ill-treatment was a genuine problem, although rarely agreeing to the fact that it was systemic. Minister of Justice Türk, in the Ecevit government, broke new ground when acknowledging in Parliament in early 2002 that torture was a problem. It was starting to be addressed in a new, more open manner. Sweeping official denial became less prevalent. The downward trend of the number of cases of torture or ill-treatment was confirmed by the EU in its annual progress report in 2007. Impunity of human rights violations, though, remains a problem, especially in cases of allegations against members of security forces.

Human rights organizations

The two sister organizations, the Human Rights Association and the Human Rights Foundation of Turkey were the leading, local human rights organizations in Turkey. They mainly focused on combating the

---

1. Article 17/3.

use of torture and rehabilitating torture victims. The Human Rights Foundation was treating up to 1,000 victims a year.[1] When I visited its office in Ankara, predominantly staffed by voluntary doctors, their concern for my constant coughing was touching since we were preoccupied with much more important things: looking through the annual reports, including some horrific pictures of torture victims. My almost five years of work on torture and other human rights issues at the UN in Geneva had me well prepared but it was still unsettling. There is such a difference between being out in the field, coming face to face with reality, and negotiating conventions and resolutions.

The branch offices of the two human rights organizations were often forced to close by the authorities for varied periods of time. Their staff lived a dangerous existence. Their freedom, sometimes even their lives, were at stake. Several incidents took place over the years when documents, such as medical journals, were confiscated. One of the founders and former chairman of the Human Rights Association, established in 1986, was a well-known human rights defender, Akın Birdal, with an MBA from Ankara University. He was attacked by ultra-right-wing extremists and shot in his office in spring 1999. When I visited the human rights organization two years later, located in a modest apartment on a noisy street in Ankara, the cluster of bullet holes from the gunshots was still visible in the thin door. Birdal was severely injured but miraculously survived. He was imprisoned a month afterwards, only to be released on medical grounds four months later, in autumn 1999.

For many years, a very limited number of human rights NGOs existed. It was a dangerous vocation. There was a turnaround from the beginning of the new millennium, when civil society kept growing, both in numbers and in empowerment. Their involvement, specialized knowledge and unprecedented new dialogue with decision-makers

---

1. 918 credible cases of torture and ill-treatment were reported across five of the Human Rights Foundation's branches during 2004.

made the NGOs increasingly important partners in the reform process.

Parliamentarian efforts stopped

In Parliament, a Committee on Human Rights led by the female Social Democrat Sema Piskinsüt was receiving widespread attention for its reporting on many cases of torture, based on interviews with more than 8,000 prisoners in different parts of the country. Torture chambers where special tools were being used were discovered and reported by the Committee. Piskinsüt was, however, forced to resign from the Committee in July 2001. A prosecutor accused her of hiding evidence of torture, when the Committee refused to submit a list of names of those interviewed, who had been promised anonymity. She remained in Parliament but only for about a year. Ecevit's party, the DSP, which she represented, did not get sufficient votes to remain in Parliament. When I first arrived in Ankara, shortly after she was forced to resign from the Human Rights Committee, I was recommended to pay her a courtesy visit in Parliament. It was suggested by a leading Turkish industrialist, keen to see his country reformed, and a future EU member, who vividly and with pride described her courage. Sema Piskinsüt later left the DSP Party.

Successful international monitoring

Internationally, many organizations and some countries were closely monitoring human rights development in Turkey. The use of torture and restrictions on freedom of expression dominated the agenda over a long period. Apart from the leading role of the EU, among them were the United Nations, the Council of Europe and the US.

The UN Committee on Torture presented a detailed report on Turkey in May 2003, expressing concern about the many and consistent allegations of torture and ill-treatment of detainees held in police custody. Despite many complaints, members of security forces were rarely punished. At the same time, the UN Committee welcomed some of the recent constitutional and legal reforms, which included the principle that evidence obtained through torture should not be invoked as evidence in any proceedings.

Widespread torture, beating and other abuses by security forces were reported in the US State Department's 2005 report on Turkey. Security forces most commonly tortured leftists and Kurdish rights activists, noted the US report.[1]

The Council of Europe, a Strasbourg-based organization which has Turkey as one of its founding members, carried out a special monitoring of Turkey's obligations to democracy, the rule of law and human rights by its Parliamentary Assembly. The Council also had a Committee for the Prevention of Torture, which made regular visits to Turkey and contributed to important prison reforms. After eight years of special monitoring the Committee was concluded in June 2004 and approved by an overwhelming majority. Many parliamentarians made emotional interventions on the progress that had been made in Turkey since the monitoring procedure had started in 1996. Only one parliamentarian spoke out against ceasing the procedure. As long as Turkey refused to properly address the Armenian issue it should carry on, a French parliamentarian argued, but in vain.

Human rights victims took power

As soon as the AK Party gained power, it quickly became clear that combating torture was a top priority. The party leader Erdoğan and temporary Prime Minister Gül often reminded EU meetings that they were themselves human rights victims. Their families had also suffered, going through mental torture during Erdoğan's imprisonment. 'Zero tolerance of torture' became the campaign motto of the brand-new government. The two top politicians' commitment to fight the

---

1.   US State Department Bureau of Democracy, Human Rights and Labor, *Turkey. Country Report on Human Rights Practices*, 28 February 2005.

violations and improve respect for human rights came across as very genuine and therefore convincing.

Far-reaching and sweeping legal reforms were adopted by broad consensus in Parliament. It also had an active Human Rights Investigation Committee, which travelled to different parts of the country, including prisons, to collect complaints of human rights violations. This time around it was allowed to carry on its work without any legal interference, unlike the situation in summer 2001. Crucial laws were revised or introduced. Permission from a superior in order to open investigations on public officials was no longer a requirement. Shorter custody periods were introduced. Thus, the high-risk period when many cases of violations took place was reduced.

Harsher punishment for those convicted of torture and ill-treatment was introduced. The statute of limitations for alleged perpetrators was increased to fifteen years. The changes were part of the fight against a culture of impunity. Trials against suspected torturers had been taking place since the 1960s but only recently were convictions successfully carried through. Convictions of security personnel were rare and imprisonment non-existent, something which was often criticized in meetings between EU ambassadors in Ankara and Turkish top officials. The so-called Manissa case, in which ten police officers tortured sixteen youths in the western Anatolian town of Manissa in 1996, became a symbol of impunity. Therefore, it was significant that the Supreme Court confirmed long prison sentences for the policemen in spring 2003.

Thus, tangible results were emerging. Torture and ill-treatment were diminishing. Severe forms of these practices were now rarely used and there were fewer reports of ill-treatment in detention places, according to the EU Commission in its 2005 Progress Report on Turkey. Problems still existed though. Human rights organizations expressed concern over an increase in ill-treatment outside detention places, for example in parking lots, and different kinds of abusive methods, such as sleep deprivation, which left no physical marks. The lack of independent monitoring of places of detention by national bodies is pointed out in the EU Commission report in 2007. So is the fact that victims of torture or ill-treatment have mostly to rely on NGOs for rehabilitation.

'Beatings come from heaven'

'We are a society that grows up being beaten and later in life becomes accustomed to giving beatings.' That was how the Education Minister Hüseyin Çelik expressed himself in a TV programme on violence in schools. The journalist Mehmet Ali Birand, who led the TV discussion in early 2006, suggested a change to the educational system and cultural approach, to escape the culture of violence whereby parents used to say 'beatings come from heaven.' Otherwise 'we reap what we have sown,' he warned.[1]

The successful actions taken in Turkey against torture and ill-treatment illustrate that a vicious circle of sanctioned violence can be broken, and if not eradicated then greatly reduced. Strong political will from the government, wide parliamentary support and active non-governmental organizations brought about an advanced set of provisions in this area. Together with international monitoring, particularly by the EU, this had a carrot, not only a stick, to offer and it turned out to be a winning combination. Another contributing factor was that the overall violence in society decreased dramatically after the end of the internal conflict with the PKK. There is a potential risk that the renewed PKK terrorism could lead to a deteriorating human rights situation.

A leading Turkish human rights activist, specializing in combating torture, cautioned the Swedish Foreign Minister Anna Lindh only a few weeks before the crucial decision in 1999 on whether or not Turkey should receive status as an EU candidate country. He warned that 'if Turkey becomes isolated from Europe the oppressive forces

---

1.   Mehmet Ali Birand, column in the *Turkish Daily News*, 30 March 2006.

will gain, while an EU integration process will help the progressive ones.'

Freedom of religion

'I want a church.' That was the clear message, often repeated to Prime Minister Erdoğan and Foreign Minister Gül by the Dutch ambassador Gosses in Ankara during the Dutch rotating EU Presidency in 2004. As progress was being made in combating torture, little improvement could be noticed as regards religious freedoms. Allowing a church to be built on the south coast of Turkey, around Alanya, where an increasing number of retired German and Dutch had settled, became a symbol of the need for more rights and tolerance in Turkey towards Christians and other non-Muslim communities. Compared with European standards, there are still serious limitations to religious freedom in Turkey.

In the Lausanne Treaty of 1923, the only minorities in Turkey accorded official status are the Jewish, Greek Orthodox and Armenian communities.[1] Since then, all non-Muslim religious communities have encountered various problems and inconveniences. They have ranged from problems regarding the right and recognition of real estate for non-Muslims to the granting of residence permits for foreign clergy.

Problems with the training of religious functionaries and residence permits for foreign clergy remain. I met one vicar at a large national day reception (for a European country). He was frustrated that he had had to be registered formally as administrative embassy staff when he failed to get a work permit as a clergyman from the Turkish authorities.

Thousands of Christians emigrated or fled, mainly to Germany or Sweden, from the Mardin area, near the Syrian border, during the 1980s and 1990s, leaving a tiny Christian community behind. But there is a trickle of those now wanting to return, at least for a visit.

---

1.   Articles 37–45 in the Lausanne Peace Treaty, signed and ratified in 1923.

In the EU's 2005 Progress Report on Turkey, restricted property rights and the lack of legal representation for religious minorities and communities were highlighted. The problems were still unsolved two years later. A comprehensive legislative framework in line with European standards should be adopted, urged the EU Commission. The Cave Church of St Peter in Antakya, near the Syrian border, is claimed to be where the apostle preached and to be Christianity's very first church. During a visit there in summer 2003, I found the church heartbreakingly dilapidated. During Pope Paul VI's visit to Turkey in 1968, he was promised by President Cevdet Sunay that it would be registered as a property of the Latin Catholic Church. The issue is still unresolved.

After an increase in attacks against Christians in 2007, the Ministry of Interior contacted all governors across the country requesting them to take necessary measures to prevent such attacks from happening again and to enhance tolerance towards persons with different religions. The unusual and prompt action by the government was taken shortly after vicious murders in Malatya of three Protestants at their community publishing house.

Magical monastery

A few kilometres outside Mardin, halfway up a barren mountain ridge, stands the sixth-century 'Saffron Monastery', *Deyr el-Zaferan*. The Oxford-educated Turkish bishop greeted me warmly during my first visit in 2002. He was looking after the tiny Christian community of Syrian Orthodox[1] still left in the area. Most of his community emigrated during the 1980s and 1990s. Then, the security situation was atrocious and freedom of religion highly restricted. Preceding that, the monastery's Aramaic school was closed by the Turkish authorities in 1978.

The monastery buildings were grouped around a courtyard with

1. *Süryani Kadim* in Turkish.

a cloister, where we spent the evenings drinking tea. The bedroom cells offered to visitors were predictably basic but with a beautiful view overlooking the steppes and a nearby Syrian town. With only the bishop, a couple of monks and myself as the sole visitor, it felt a bit desolate and reminiscent of times gone by.

During the next few years it was rapidly transformed. As the conflict with the PKK subsided, security improved. At the same time, freedom of religion was enhanced as the Turkish government ambitiously pursued EU reforms. More and more Assyrians-Syriacs came to visit, some from Sweden, many daring to return only after fifteen or twenty years. Churches and monasteries, which were in dire need of renovation after decades of forced neglect, were permitted by the authorities to be renovated. It was amazing to see how the small churches, which had looked beyond repair, were being restored, mainly financed by overseas communities.

Some of the Christians had problems reclaiming the properties they had left empty upon emigrating, but were given support by the local authorities to have their homes returned. During my last visit, in June 2006, the monastery was bustling with life. Daily, thousands of tourists, many of them Muslim Turks, visited the Saffron Monastery. It was undergoing a careful renovation, financed by the EU Commission. TV satellite programmes were being planned. The liturgy in the monastery's 1,400-year-old church would be broadcast across the world. The monks were skilfully managing the large daily influx of visitors ensuring that the church services and special atmosphere were not disturbed by the guided tours. The atmosphere of an abandoned sleeping beauty was gone, hopefully forever.

Progress; but how far?

It was a cold day in Istanbul in March 2003. Demonstrators against an American invasion of Iraq, expected to occur any day, were gathering in the centre, while a large number of riot police were getting prepared. One young police officer turned to a demonstrator, a human rights activist, explaining that he would also join in if he were off duty. 'His unexpected frankness towards me, a complete stranger, proved that Turkey has changed and will never be the same again.' This was recalled by a young activist from Istanbul, a friend of mine, who as an academic researcher on Kurdish women in the southeast had had to learn to live for years with harassment from security personnel.

While other former EU candidate countries in central and eastern Europe achieved democracy in a relatively short period, Turkey has had an entirely different history; a pluralistic democracy since the 1950s, interrupted by military coups, a long and violent internal conflict and serious human rights deficiencies. Many problems still remain, among them the implementation of the new laws and limitations on freedom of expression. Nevertheless, it does not change the fact that what Turkey has achieved since 2001 is unprecedented in its own history as well as in that of the region.

SIX

The Kurdish Question:
A Roadblock to Turkish EU membership?

When tourists are preparing themselves for an evening out at the thriving holiday destination of Bodrum on the Aegean coastline, which is like any fashionable French Riviera resort, the sun casts an orange glow over Turkey's ancient East, more than 1,600 kilometres away. It is a world apart. A Kurdish-dominated, poverty-stricken region which is more like neighbouring Iran, Iraq and Syria than the European Mediterranean ambiance of Turkey's coastal resorts. When I first landed in the regional centre of Diyarbakir in the southeast on a freezing winter's day in 2002, I felt a sense of déjà vu, as though I was back in oriental, Middle Eastern surroundings. One difference here were the two local policemen on guard all night outside my room at Dedeman's, an austere hotel where the few foreigners who came to visit usually stayed, at a time when emergency rule still prevailed. The hotel overlooked the office of the mayor of Diyarbakir, who traditionally represented a pro-Kurdish party, at the time HADEP. In this part of Turkey, an estimated 85–90 per cent of the population is Kurdish with judges, military, teachers and other state employees making up the remaining part.

The fifteen years of violent conflict between the state and the separatist organization PKK started in 1984 and contributed significantly to the underdevelopment and widespread poverty found in the Kurdish areas of the southeast and eastern parts of the country. So did emergency rule, which was only completely lifted on 30 November 2002. Increasing attacks in 2007, amounting to several hundreds, by the PKK and other terrorist organizations led to a deterioration of the situation, resulting in the establishment of three security zones along the border with Iraq. Not even a prestigious, multi-billion-dollar governmental project has managed to erase a longstanding grievance about unemployment, social discrimination and lack of commitment from different central governments to develop the region. Every autumn, all foreign ambassadors in Ankara were invited to go as a group to the 'Southeastern Anatolian project', which is well-known under its Turkish acronym 'GAP' since its launch in the 1980s. It aims to change the socio-economic structure of the region, stretching from Kiliş on the Syrian border to Şirnak in the east, near the Iraqi border, by increasing income levels and living standards. There is still a very long way to go.

The overwhelming unemployment and the fact that 60 per cent of the population (2006 statistics) live in absolute poverty in the southeast and eastern provinces of Anatolia, the area's official name, reflects the huge regional discrepancies and problems, which are a recurrent topic in EU–Turkey talks. The internally displaced population, estimated at around one million people, is one aspect of the problem, and is a consequence of the long conflict and forced evacuations during the 1980s and 1990s. According to an official report by a Turkish parliamentary committee in 1997, the Turkish military forced the evacuation of more than 3,800 villages, which were destroyed or burnt in the Kurdish areas as part of the efforts to combat the PKK.

Today several obstacles, apart from the obvious economic reasons such as poor or non-existent infrastructure and difficulties in making a living, mean that there are only a trickle of returnees. The controversial village guards system is still in use. Launched in the 1980s, the system involved local Kurdish men employed by the military to protect their villages from the PKK, but in reality they were often used as support troops by the military to attack other villages during the conflict. Some of them repeatedly overstepped their authority, harassing or abusing returnees or neighbouring villagers. The EU's strong recommendation to dismantle the system has not yet been implemented. The state employs around 57,000 village guards according to official 2007 figures. One governor explained to me that the village guards were being phased out either through normal retirement or by being forced to resign upon reports of abuse – although a few years later (in 2007), there were cases of new voluntary village guards being hired, who were not paid but armed by the state.

Reluctance to leave city life and return to an often remote, rural area is another reason for the limited return of many of those who have been internally displaced. Many prefer to carry on living in cities like Diyarbakir, which has taken the brunt of the internally displaced population. However, among those who might prefer to return, some have no villages left to go back to.

As an official EU candidate country from 1999, the EU's financial assistance to Turkey was initially quite modest. 'We only receive as much pre-accession financial assistance from the EU as Malta does,' said one frustrated Turkish top civil servant to me in 2003. Since then, it has multiplied considerably and Turkey's share amounted to 500 million Euro in 2006. But recent figures show that the GDP in Turkey's eastern provinces lags conspicuously behind. Compared to the average GDP among the twenty-five EU member states, it corresponds to only between 7 and 16 per cent (that was prior to the EU entry of Bulgaria and Romania on 1 January 2007).

The Kurdish-speaking population has migrated in large numbers from eastern to western Turkey, to cities like Istanbul and Ankara. Istanbul, which now has an estimated three million inhabitants of

Kurdish origin within its sprawling city boundaries, is emerging as a centre of Kurdish culture in Turkey.

Only a few years ago the ban on the Kurdish language, linguistically connected to Farsi, was lifted in Turkey. Since the early days of the founding of the nation, ethnicity was viewed as a threat against the integrity of the republic. To reduce ethnic differences became a state policy. As a result, the official position on the Kurdish languages was clear-cut for decades. It was repeatedly described as only a dialect, not a language. That was still the case in early 2002, when a Swedish parliamentary delegation was visiting a top civil servant in Ankara. 'Kurdish only consists of six hundred words. In addition, it would be impossible to meet the demands of Kurdish-speaking people since there are sixteen different mother tongues in Turkey,' the official explained. Children with a mother tongue other than Turkish, for example Kurdish, cannot be taught their mother tongue in the public school system. This is only possible through private tuition, but all private courses in Kurdish were closed down in 2004 for lack of demand.

In September 2004, the state radio and TV channels started to broadcast in Kurdish, as well as other minority languages such as Bosnian, Arabic and some local languages as part of the reform drive, but still with strict time limitations. Four local radio and TV stations were broadcasting in Kurdish in 2007. Films and music programmes are excluded from the time restrictions.

In a change from only a few years ago, Kurdish literature and music products can now be displayed in the windows of book stores such as those along the well-known pedestrian *Istiklal Caddesi* (Independence Avenue), which cuts through the old European quarters of Istanbul. Awareness of the Kurdish language is gradually spreading beyond its own circles. Many in Turkey would be surprised to know that there are different Kurdish languages being spoken in Turkey (*Kurmanji*) and in neigbouring northern Iraq (*Sorani*) as well as different alphabets being used (Latin and Arabic).

The Kurdish question has cast a huge shadow over EU–Turkish relations for many years.[1] Even mentioning the word 'Kurd' could result in an angry reaction from Turkish politicians or civil servants. Representing, as I did, a government which does not shy away from emphasizing the importance of human rights, including those of Kurds, could result in unexpected and emotional reactions from Turkish officials, even at small dinner parties (which to a diplomat is less than twenty people). I had briefly mentioned this to my father, who visited me in Ankara in 2002, but he thought that I had to be exaggerating. So when my father accompanied me to a dinner at a Gulf Arab colleague's exquisite residence, he was taken aback by the outburst that I faced from a senior Turkish official as I was introducing myself to him for the first time. The Swedish government was obviously not his favourite, to say the least.

These frictions were exposed publicly, for far from the first time, in April 2002 when an agitated political debate erupted over a map of Turkey, which mentioned 'Kurdistan'. It was published in the Swedish daily *Aftonbladet* in its travel section on Turkey. The credit-card-sized map described the 500,000-square-kilometre area across Turkey, Iraq, Iran and Syria as 'Kurdistan', where an estimated fifty million Kurds live. The Deputy Speaker of the Turkish Parliament, Mehmet Sökmenoğlu of the far-right MHP Party, demanded that the Swedish government took action against the newspaper.

The controversy became front-page news in the largest Turkish daily, *Hürriyet*. Upon being summoned to the Foreign Ministry in Ankara, I referred to the importance of press freedom. Meanwhile, the Turkish ambassador in Stockholm, Selim Kuneralp, explained eloquently in an article in the same Swedish newspaper why the map was unfortunate from a Turkish perspective, using history as a point of departure. Publishing a map with 'Kurdistan' was wrong,

---

1.   See previous chapter on human rights.

awakening tragic memories and causing dismay. Sweden must not give the impression of not respecting Turkey's territorial integrity, he argued; but he was dismissed and viciously criticized by some major Turkish media for being 'too mild' in his response.

Few Turks living in the western parts of Turkey have ever visited the mainly Kurdish-dominated areas in eastern and southern Anatolia. Those originating from there or having done their military service in the southeast and eastern parts were the most common exceptions. A mixture of apprehension about the security situation and a sense of alienation towards an entirely different kind of life prevented many from considering travelling there.

I explored those parts of the country extensively and was met with plenty of curiosity and questions upon returning to Ankara. It felt a bit strange for me, as a foreigner, to describe impressions of their own country, although I was always delighted to do so. The Kurdish women's vulnerable situation left the starkest memories.[1] The much-publicised girls' education campaign, though, gave a glimpse of hope for women's future. It became a success, with 62,000 girls enrolled in primary schools in 2005, who otherwise would not have been in school. Many of those girls live in the indigent southeast. But it will take time to eradicate the high illiteracy rate among women – one in every five – in Turkey.

An Istanbul-born friend, who is a successful career woman and a compassionate person, is privately sponsoring the education of a few girls living near Diyarbakir in the southeast, an area she has never been to and from families she has never met or known personally. However, she was a bit disappointed with the academic results of one of the girls. After contacting the school, it confirmed that the girl was properly attending thanks to the financial contribution sent to her family, which encouraged the family to let the girl get a primary education. The problem was that the girl kept fainting in class due to malnutrition, was unable to concentrate as a result and was therefore

---

1. See following chapter on women's role in society.

underachieving. My friend was shocked to learn about the conditions in her own country.

Generally, girls have a starkly subordinate position to boys, especially in poor, conservative areas. Many women are illiterate but some that I met were clearly committed to providing a better life for their offspring despite extremely limited resources. They did not want to see their daughters ending up without an education and being married off as underage brides the way some of them had been. 'Nor will I ever allow my children to marry a first cousin the way I did,' said one Kurdish woman I met in the southeast, who had first-hand experience of the serious health problems that can occur as a consequence of marrying a close relative, which is still not uncommon in the region. Her remarks were made in front of her extended family, without any reservation or shyness, and she was not contradicted by her husband or any of his brothers. They all shared a large villa in Mardin, perched on a cliff, with different flats for each family but all of them having joint finances. That fascinated me, coming from a country where individuality and independence is treasured to the point that some married couples prefer to keep their finances separate.

One trip to Turkey's most remote regions in the east brought me to towns along the Syrian, Iraqi and Iranian borders in the summer of 2004. In meetings with local officials, lawyers and NGOs, the message was encouraging. The overall human rights situation had improved noticeably as a result of the EU reforms. The previously widespread use of torture could no longer be described as systematic although there were still some cases of torture. Changed rules, the right to consult a lawyer and to contact next of kin had contributed to the improvements. But some NGOs complained that torture had moved out of police stations to parking lots and other 'out of sight' places. One defence lawyer in a border town near Iraq was concerned over the lack of hope for the future, with no jobs available whatsoever. Some young boys, only thirteen to fourteen years old, ran away from home to 'go up into the mountains', a synonym for joining the PKK, leaving desperately unhappy mothers behind. As a last resort, they turned to a well-connected and respected lawyer in the hope of getting help to bring their sons back home.

Winding roads on the two-three-thousand-metre-high mountains to Hakkari, a small province positioned at the juncture of Iran and Iraq, offered spectacular views over the steep-sided gorges. Kurdish women in colourful ankle-length dresses walked alongside almost empty roads. The only foreigners I spotted during my almost week-long visit in the region were a German, hippie-looking couple in their sixties driving a beat-up, orange Volkswagen bus. They had discovered what must be one of the most spectacular and untouched areas of Turkey. 'If all the mountains were flattened, this province would have the same surface area as Sweden,' governor Erdoğan Gürbuz noted. I certainly believed him after the precipitous zigzag roads I had travelled on to get there.

He described the illegal but profitable cross-border trade going on, which was difficult to stop due to the inaccessibility of the area. Donkeys were trained to walk across the mountains into Iraq, where they were kept a few days without food. They were then heavily loaded with oil barrels. Keen to return home, where hay was waiting, they walked back on paths human beings could hardly pass.

The potential of border areas as future tourism and trade centres was highlighted in a recent report on 'Social and Economic Priorities for the Eastern and South Eastern Anatolia Regions' by UNDP and the respected Turkish Foundation on Economic and Social Studies (TESEV) in November 2006. Public investment on a large scale has to be initiated in the neglected infrastructure, health and education sectors. Community-driven campaigns are crucial, underlined the report.

During my travels, a new openness among governors was noticeable, compared to my visits there only a few years earlier. They were keen to talk about their provinces and EU human rights reforms and did not shy away from discussing problems. The majority of the governors were recent appointees by the AK Party government, which was keen to get a fresh start in the region. The governors are career civil servants with considerable influence and power. They faced particular challenges in the Kurdish areas, where security remained a problem and where the implementation of the new, strengthened human rights legislation met with many obstacles from the judiciary. Among them were the State Security Courts, later abolished.

My next stop was for meetings in the town of Van, on the shore of Europe's largest lake with the same name. On entering the governor's office building, there was a huge colour photo of a Van cat in the frugal foyer. It had one blue eye and one yellow eye, being a unique breed of white cats. The meeting itself was as usual quite formal – anything else would have been strange considering the serious and delicate questions on the agenda – but I could not resist interposing and telling him proudly that my family had just got a kitten in Ankara, who was of mixed heritage but partly of Van origin. These cats are world-famous (as I learnt in Turkey) not only for their different-coloured eyes but also for their love of swimming.

The Van governor, Hikmet Tan, appeared worn, having served for several years in such a high security posting and in one of the poorest among the country's eighty-one provinces. Only days after our meeting, his convoy was attacked with road bombs. His bodyguard was killed and several people were injured but the governor survived unharmed.

After almost six years of lull in the conflict, there was renewed violence in 2005 between the army and the PKK, which by then had been renamed a couple of times to KADEK and later Kongra-Gel (Kurdistan People's Congress), although its original name was frequently still in use. The PKK had declared unilateral ceasefires three times since 1994 and a fourth time in autumn 2006. By then attacks had intensified and more than one hundred soldiers and four hundred civilians were killed that year. The upsurge of unrest sparked fears not only of a return to separatist conflict but also that it could create further obstacles on an already bumpy road to Europe. The EU decision in spring 2003 to officially declare the PKK as terrorists by putting it on the EU list of terrorist organizations was met with widespread praise and approval in Turkey although many thought it was also long overdue. I had strangers come up to me at conferences and social events thanking me, as an ambassador from an EU member state, for that decision. Yet again, I was taken by surprise by the involvement with which ordinary citizens followed EU matters.

The political environment had transformed in the Kurdish areas. There was a general, strong support for democracy and Turkish EU membership rather than separatism or demands for independence. When I recalled these impressions upon my return to Ankara they were often met with scepticism among Turkish colleagues and friends. The mutual mistrust runs deep after a long history of recurrent conflicts going back to the early days of modern Turkey.

'Equal citizenship' is a favoured expression among Kurds, assuming that it would be best safeguarded by Turkey being a full EU member. 'Minority rights', on the other hand, is a contentious expression since the notion of minority has a negative connotation in Turkey. It has implied second-rate citizens since the early days of the republic when the 1923 Lausanne Treaty only granted minority status to three non-Muslim groups. Up till then Kurds had enjoyed certain rights.

Support for EU membership was remarkably strong across Turkey during the years preceding the start of membership talks in October 2005, lingering at around 75 per cent for a long time. Meanwhile, it was even stronger in the Kurdish area, reaching 90 per cent, reflecting expectations of further cultural rights and freedoms granted with Turkey on track for its EU bid. It also illustrates the evolution away from the PKK's core objectives of separatism. The PKK has since dropped its demands for an independent country and focuses on other issues, such as ending the solitary confinement of their leader Öcalan and obtaining a general amnesty for their militants.

The 'Kurdish question' was acknowledged in a historic visit to Diyarbakir by Prime Minster Erdoğan in August 2005, he himself being a representative from the southeastern town of Siirt (although he originates from the northeastern part of the country). He indicated in his positive speech that great states are those which learn from their mistakes.

'Sixty members of parliament from the ruling party are Kurds,' said Ali Babacan, a rising star in the Cabinet and Turkey's chief negotiator for EU affairs, during a meeting in Stockholm in November 2006. He noted it in passing, without any further reflection. About 180 parliamentarians of a total of 550 elected in 2002 were Kurdish. Most reformed laws were in place. The key was now to have them implemented, he stressed at a meeting in the Swedish Parliament. 'We know we are being closely monitored, which is OK.'

Şeraffin Elci, a leading Kurdish intellectual and former Cabinet minister, was the first senior politician to officially bring up his Kurdish identity in the late 1970s, causing a major controversy. Despite this, there are several examples of assimilated Kurds among top Turkish politicians. Turgut Özal was the first prime minister to speak publicly about his Kurdish origins. He initiated a more liberal approach towards the Kurds. In 1991 (by then Turgut Özal had become president), legislation (Article 2932) was altered, putting an end to the ban on speaking Kurdish. But the escalation of violence in the conflict between the PKK and the army, combined with the president's sudden death in 1993, put a de facto end at the time to the liberalization of the Kurdish issue. It would take another ten years before there was renewed impetus.

It was during Turgut Özal's time that the two Kurdish leaders in northern Iraq, Jalal Talabani and Massoud Barzani, were issued red, VIP Turkish passports, enabling them to travel easily and at times mediate between the PKK and the Turkish state. Both visited Ankara regularly. Years later, they sometimes met with the EU ambassadors while in Ankara. One of those meetings was held in a small conference room at the Hilton hotel, not long before the US-led invasion of Iraq in spring 2003. I assume that no one at the time expected that the man sitting in front of us would become the first president in the post-Saddam era. When the sixty-two-year-old Talabani, who has been an advocate for Kurdish rights and democracy since the age of thirteen, was elected president of Iraq in April 2005, it was a historic appointment.

The overall socio-economic situation remains precarious in the southeast, while hopes pinned to improving the political circumstances have been increasingly undermined. The recent upsurge in violence and the ultra-nationalist backlash against the AK Party government, accusing it of being too soft on a number of issues such as the PKK, Iraqi Kurds and the EU, have hampered further progress. The fact that there are no obvious Kurdish interlocutors for the government has resulted in almost non-existent dialogue between the authorities and the locally-elected politicians. Furthermore, the 10 per cent threshold necessary to be elected into Parliament is unlikely to be changed any time soon. Therefore, chances of pro-Kurdish political parties with local strongholds making it into national politics remain slim, but by standing as independent candidates in the last general elections more than twenty Kurdish nationalists could enter Parliament.

The success of the Iraqi Kurds in setting up an autonomous and prosperous area in the northern parts since 2003 has been met with quiet acceptance on the Turkish government's side. But the continuation of the PKK insurgencies into Turkey from bases in northern Iraq is putting immense internal pressure on the government in Ankara. It is also straining relations, especially with the US, whose forces are giving priority to other more pressing issues, such as preventing an all-out civil war in Iraq. Turkey's nightmare is an independent Kurdish state emerging in northern Iraq as the rest of Iraq descends into a lengthy sectarian, civil war, threatening Turkey's own territorial unity.

A few days after the historic elections of the AK Party in

November 2002, I was received by Tayyip Erdoğan, and congratulated him on behalf of my government for the election victory. I also requested him to permit the Swedish Foreign Minister Anna Lindh to visit southeastern Turkey, something which she had de facto been prevented from doing for some time by the previous government, as had other foreign, top politicians. Mr Erdoğan said, without hesitation: 'Why shouldn't she?' There is nothing to hide. But he said he had one condition. 'I want Anna Lindh to return after one year so she can notice the changes,' the future premier said with a confident smile. Anna Lindh happily committed herself to do so but was unable to fulfil his request as her life was cut short. Her successor's visit to Diyarbakir in October 2004 coincided with the publication of the EU's progress report on Turkey, surrounded by massive international attention, paving the way for Turkey's entry into membership talks.

The Turkish government has in a relatively short period managed to break the taboo and address the Kurdish issue. Important and sometimes groundbreaking reforms have been undertaken together with a cautious reconciliation process. This was reflected in the election results in 2007 when the AK Party won almost 54 per cent of the votes in the predominately Kurdish areas of south-east Turkey, well above the 47 per cent support in the country as a whole. It was an impressive mark of support for the government's reform work. It also showed a preference for equal rights and not separatism among the population in the Kurdish regions. Nevertheless, the Kurdish issue remains a hurdle, both domestically and on the road to joining the EU.

SEVEN

Women Between Tradition and Transformation

'Humankind is made up of two entities: man and woman. How could it be possible for the whole to progress if we let one half progress and neglect the other? How could it be thought possible that one half should reach the height of the skies when we let the other half wallow in shallow ground?'
Mustafa Kemal Atatürk, *Vakit* newspaper, 30 March 1923

The unfinished revolution

Women's advancement was part of Atatürk's far-reaching modernization project. The emancipation of women was viewed as one of the main requisites of a larger social revolution. A secular Civil Code was adopted in 1926, almost identical to the Swiss one, which replaced the Islamic law and created a major change in women's lives. Polygamy was banned as one element of the new legislation. The segregation between men and women was less pronounced and women became more visible in the public sphere. This is regarded as one of the most important breaking points between Ottoman society and the newly founded Turkish Republic.

Although men and women became equals before the law in Turkey more than eighty years ago, many of the new rights in practice have only benefited a few privileged women, mainly from large cities. Over the years I have met many Turks, among them successful diplomats, who – during discussions on women's position in Turkey – recounted how their mothers or grandmothers were medical doctors or academics.

Education plays a key role

The number of women with higher education has indeed been impressive for a long time. Today around 30 per cent of architects, doctors and professors are women. But despite primary education being compulsory since the early days of the Republican revolution, the number of illiterate women remains high. Men's literacy rate, which at 94 per cent[1] is considerably higher than women's, is helped by the compulsory military service. Men who cannot read are taught upon entry into the army.

The compulsory primary education was increased to eight years in 2000, but it is estimated that 600,000 girls on the whole do not attend school, according to the UN Children's Fund (UNICEF), which launched a campaign together with the Turkish government in 2003 to promote girls' education. The coordinator of the campaign in Van province, near the Iranian border, said in a recent interview that 30 per cent of girls in the poor, rural and mainly Kurdish southeast still do not attend primary school.[2]

The most common reason given for keeping girls at home is economics. Children are often viewed as a labour asset, especially girls, as a domestic help in the family home or to work in the fields alongside relatives. Although the age limit for child labour increased from twelve to fifteen years more than thirty years ago, there are still

---

1. Compared to women's 77 per cent, according to UNICEF's statistics for 2000.
2. *Turkish Daily News* (TDN), 'Village pressures keep Turkish girls from school', 6 July 2006.

a significant number of children below the age of fifteen who are employed, particularly in small enterprises and in agriculture. Thus, they are denied the right to education as prescribed in the European Social Charter,[1] as the EU Commission pointed out in its 2004 Progress Report on Turkey.

During a 2003 visit to Siirt in the southeast, the governor explained to me how a small financial incentive was paid to poor families to encourage them to send girls to school. The district governor in Diyarbakir described to me how he personally travelled to some remote villages to persuade families to send their girls to school. The Turkish government and UNICEF's campaign was fruitful, resulting in a significant increase in girls attending school.[2]

Imams, who are employed by the governmental body, the Religious Affairs Directorate, and are thus civil servants, were instructed not to perform religious marriages prior to a civil ceremony in early 2004. Many unofficial, religious ceremonies concealed polygamy. Children born out of wedlock were not registered and were therefore outside the system. Officially they simply did not exist.

'Men often take a second wife when the first one has had six to eight children and is approaching thirty years of age. Even a third wife is occasionally taken on some years later and another set of children arrive. A man's status is sometimes judged upon the size of his clan.' This was explained to me by a young governor in a poverty-stricken small town in the southeast, which I visited in the summer of 2003. Although polygamy has been forbidden since the early days of the Republic it still exists, particularly in poor, rural and remote areas. 'When I encourage them to have smaller families to give their children a better quality of life, including enabling all daughters to go to school, I am accused of trying to minimize the number of Kurds in the country,' sighed the top state official in the region. He

---

1. Article 7 of the European Social Charter, which guarantees social and economic human rights. It was adopted by the Council of Europe in 1961, revised in 1996. Turkey ratified the Charter in 1989.
2. 15 per cent on average (i.e. 19 per cent in Siirt and 11 per cent in Van) in 2004.

was nevertheless unperturbed in his optimism about the rapid EU reforms transforming his country.

In traditional and conservative regions, such as parts of the southeast, there are other obstacles, apart from poverty, to girls' education. Families' concern about their daughters' reputations makes them reluctant to let them out of sight, including going to school. The ban on headscarves in schools has also had consequences. A headmaster in Van estimated that at least 15 per cent more girls would attend if the teachers did not need to tell girls to take off their headscarves upon entering the primary school.[1] Early marriage is another problem. In addition, domesticity is often more valued by parents than academic skills for their daughters. Currently, around eight million women, or 20 per cent, in Turkey are illiterate, which is by far the highest figure among all European countries.[2]

Turkish women in the workforce: Different trends from the EU

Migration from rural areas to the cities has had a considerable effect on women's lives. From the 1960s the number of women starting to work outside the home increased noticeably. In the late 1990s, women made up one third of the overall workforce of Turkey. The deep economic crises around the turn of the millennium and high unemployment had noticeable and lingering effects on women in the workforce. While the rate of women in employment is rising in the EU, it is decreasing in Turkey. Currently, only 26 per cent of women in Turkey are part of the labour force, which is one of the lowest rates in the Organisation for Economic Cooperation and Development (OECD) area.

In Ankara, many women confused me initially when they said they were retired civil servants, despite being only in their early forties. It turned out that a generous pension package, introduced in the late 1990s, enabled employees to retire after only twenty years'

1. TDN, 6 July 2006.
2. UNDP Report on Human Development Indicators, 2005.

service in the public sector. Some of the women then chose to have a second child, but the majority of women I met in Ankara had only one child.

Women in politics

In Ankara, I was continually surprised at how few professional women I met. Moving in political circles as a diplomat, it was striking how limited women's representation was. With only twenty-five women among 550 seats in Parliament (4.4 per cent), it was lower than in any other country in the EU and lower than in countries such as Syria and Jordan. In the 2007 general election, though, the number of female legislators almost doubled to 51, bringing the proportion of women in Parliament to 9 per cent. Only twenty-five female mayors were elected in the 2004 local elections compared to 3,209 male mayors. Prime Minister Erdoğan has tried to tackle this situation by requesting the AK Party's provincial offices to increase the number of women active in politics. The male hegemony in politics is not due to a lack of enthusiasm on behalf of women but to men stopping women from joining politics, the Prime Minister believed.

A senior delegation of exclusively female politicians from Sweden visited several cities, from Istanbul in the west to Batman in the east in spring 2005. Meetings with the local AK Party branches in Diyarbakir, where I was accompanying them, were remarkably well-attended and the many questions on the EU, democracy and women's rights reflected a keen interest and self-assurance among the local women. There seemed to be no lack of potential politicians among them.

Celebrating suffrage rights in Konya

Shortly after moving to Turkey, I was visiting Konya, the capital of the ancient Selçuk kingdom and Turkey's most important religious centre in the heartland of Anatolia. The huge, modern Selçuk University with 50,000 students on the vast Anatolian steppe arranged a seminar to celebrate the anniversary of the suffrage rights introduced in 1934. This was a few years after Britain but ten years earlier than in France. I was invited to speak on 'Women in the world: A Swedish perspective'.

In Turkey, the custom is that the most senior speaker talks towards the end, unlike in Western Europe or the US. This time it was State Minister Gemici, who shared illustrative information. Female representatives in Parliament accounted for 4.6 per cent in the elections of 1935, only to remain at that same, low level sixty-seven years later. Local elections (in 1999) turned out even lower levels; around 1.5 per cent of the elected officials were women. The Minister stressed that 'Provision of equality means to a certain extent a completion of the enlightenment reforms of Atatürk'.[1]

Some travel guides caution foreign women before visiting the deeply pious and Muslim stronghold of Konya, but during my several visits there I was met by nothing but warm hospitality and pride in sharing its rich history. What I remember most vividly, apart from the magnificent Mevlana Museum,[2] was that all 2,000 students attending the seminar on suffrage rights remained quiet in a hot auditorium for four hours without a break. My eldest daughter, a freshman at a Swedish university, who had accompanied me to Konya, remarked that that kind of discipline would have been unthinkable at her university.

An academic on oppression

Despite the Kemalist reforms of the 1920s, Turkish women still face oppression. The reasons are 'a Mediterranean culture with its honour

---

1. State Minister Hasan Gemici (in the Ecevit government) at a seminar on 'The 67th Anniversary of the Acquisition of Political Rights of Turkish Women', 7 December 2001.
2. Including the tomb of Celaleddin Rumi (Mevlana), 1207–1273, the mystical poet and founder of the Sufi sect and the Whirling Dervishes. More than 1.5 million Muslims a year, mainly Turkish, make a pilgrimage there.

and shame codes, the Islamic tradition with its divine judgment on female behaviour and the Kemalist ideology with its stereotype of an asexual, self-sacrificing Turkish woman,'[1] according to the academic Meltem Müftüler-Baç. Legal equality, granted to Turkish women since the early days of the Republic, has failed to result in their emancipation, she argues.

Since this analysis was presented in 1999, further reforms enhancing women's rights have been introduced. In addition, there are enough high-profile Turkish women in academia, business, diplomacy and civil society for them to be an anomaly as well as an inspiration among Muslim societies. The two Ankara professors Feride Acar and Yakin Ertürk, who work internationally on women's rights, Solmaz Ünaydin, one of Turkey's first female ambassadors, the businesswoman Mrs Semahat Arsel in Istanbul and the founder of a leading women's organization in Diyarbakir, Mrs Nebahat Akkoç, are just a few of many impressive women whom I met during my years in Turkey.

Killings in the name of 'honour'

Güldünya was a twenty-two-year-old girl from Bitlis, a small, old town east of Diyarbakir. She was pregnant and unmarried and as a result her family sent her away. She gave birth and named her baby *Umut* (Hope). But after she had supposedly besmirched her family's honour, her two brothers tried to kill her, shooting her in the middle of the street in Istanbul. As Güldünya was recovering in a hospital bed from the attempt on her life, her brothers returned and killed her, following a family decision, in February 2004. Public uproar followed in Turkey. It also received much attention in Europe, where some, however, used it as a pretext for arguing that Turkey was unfit to join the EU.

Güldünya became a symbol of the 'honour' killing, which is a

---

1.   Meltem Müftüler-Baç, 'Turkish Women's Predicament', in *Women's Studies International Forum*, vol. 22, no. 3, 1999, pp. 303–315.

planned execution by immediate family members of girls or women. From time immemorial, a family's honour has been associated with a daughter's virginity and chaste behaviour in Mediterranean countries, Turkey included, and in the Middle East. A girl or a woman believed to have overstepped cultural or traditional limits could be victim of an 'honour' killing. The act of choosing her own husband rather than accepting her family's choice would be one such example.

The Turkish media, which had highlighted the problem at length, wrote extensively about the murder of the young woman. The Religious Affairs Directorate (*Diyanet*), which oversees Muslim religious facilities and education, reacted immediately. Its president, Professor Bardakoğlu, strongly condemned 'honour' killings as 'one of the most extreme manifestations of widespread violence against women.' It is caused by numerous factors, but religion is not one of them, he underlined in a statement.[1] Instead, the practice of a patriarchal mentality with 'a way of thinking that gives priority to and revolves around the existence and rights of men', was largely made responsible. The imams, who are employed by the *Diyanet* and are therefore civil servants, were instructed to condemn 'honour' killings. As a result, that urgent request was conveyed in Friday prayers in 75,000 mosques across the country. 'To have the head of the Religious Affairs Ministry seeing women's rights as important may in itself bring about change,' said the Turkish professor Yakin Ertürk,[2] who is the respected UN Special Rapporteur on violence against women. She welcomed the way in which millions of men attending Friday prayers could be reached by the imams, in a way that human rights advocates often cannot.

The majority of suicides committed in the Diyarbakir region were in fact 'honour' killings executed by family members of the victims.[3]

---

1. President of the Religious Affairs Directorate, press release, 8 March 2004.
2. Catherine Collins, 'Reforms preached in 70,000 mosques', *Tribune*, 9 May 2004.
3. Speech by EU Commission Ambassador Kretschmer on 'The Turkish Penal Code and Gender Equality', Ankara, 10 December 2003; references to research

Batman, one and a half hours' drive from Diyarbakir, was labelled 'City of Suicide', which prompted the UN Special Rapporteur to make a special fact-finding mission in May 2006.

She found several key factors contributing to suicides in the region, among them forced and early marriages, domestic violence and denial of reproductive rights. Rapid socio-economic change, poverty and displacement were other factors.[1]

Batman, a bleak, modern town in southeast Anatolia, has grown from a village to a sprawling town after becoming one of the main crude oil production centres, following the discovery of oil in 1948. When I stayed with an extended Kurdish family in Batman during some stiflingly hot days in June 2006, they agreed with the UN findings. The rapid urbanization had changed women's lives. Women had become more isolated in their new homes in anonymous apartment blocks and thus more dependent on their families compared to their previous lives in villages. I was surprised and encouraged at how openly the men, as well as the women I met discussed the suicides and 'honour' killings in their home town.

As I was leaving town to fly back alone to Ankara, my host family found a distant relative, after many phone calls, who was booked on the same plane as me. Whether he was there to keep me company or to escort me, since I was travelling unaccompanied, would have depended on who you asked. I just enjoyed the friendly company.

No More 'if onlys'

It was a bitingly cold day in Diyarbakir in winter 2002. I had left Ankara behind, covered in snow, and flown an hour and a half southeast to Diyarbakir, and a quick walk along the city's massive,

---

by Dicle University, Diyarbakir, for the period of 1998–2003 when 134 cases of suicide occurred.

1. UN press release from the Special Rapporteur of the UN Commission on Human Rights on violence against women, its causes and consequences, 31 May 2006.

black walls, which many of the relatively few visitors like to do, was not very tempting. Allegedly, they are the world's second longest after the Great Wall of China. I was on my way to visit an organization, KA-MER (Women's Centre), which was housed in a modest, two-story house, brimming with various activities. It was a place where threatened and abused women learned about their rights and picked up new skills. Clothes as well as colourful gift boxes were handmade and sold, a telephone helpline gave guidance and support and a small restaurant on the ground floor helped to finance the activities.

The former teacher Nebahat Akkoç, who founded the organization in 1997, introduced me to her small staff, all women, and some with painful personal experiences. Mrs Akkoç, herself a widow, had decided to launch a project to combat killings in the name of 'honour' through preventive measures as well as assisting victims with psychological and legal counselling. She had a low-key manner but her strength and dedication were obvious.

A young, illiterate woman, Şemse Allak, from a village outside Mardin, was a victim of stoning. Her relatives tried to kill her after she became pregnant out of wedlock but she survived the initial attack. Her fate left an unforgettable imprint on the founder of KA-MER. Şemse became the first person to be treated under the new project.

After a few days travelling around in the region for various meetings, I returned to Ankara to prepare for the Swedish foreign minister's visit to Turkey the following month. I brought with me beautiful gift boxes in light purple silk, made by the women at KA-MER, to the delight of my youngest daughter, twelve at the time, who had only white and lilac in her bedroom. I did not have the heart to explain to her what I had learnt about the cruelty against women, that they were being killed by their own relatives and that the murders were often instigated and encouraged by the victims' own mothers. When Foreign Minister Anna Lindh visited KA-MER a month later, in February 2003, she became the first to lend her support to the pilot project. Her announcement of political and financial support was made to a large crowd of journalists, who for the first time in over a decade had a foreign top official's visit in the area to cover. An aura of enthusiasm and anticipation of better times ahead for women was felt in the air in KA-MER's combined dining room and tiny restaurant, which was packed with people who had managed to squeeze in.

KA-MER's founder recalled how the victim of the stoning, Şemse Allak, later died from her injuries and that the murder of Anna Lindh took place the same year. How poignant it is that the paths of these two women crossed in a village in southeast Anatolia only a short time before the deaths of both, Mrs Akkoç wrote in a book on killings in the name of 'honour' entitled *No More 'if onlys'*. However, she ended on a generally positive note: Turkey is changing fast and women are becoming active proponents of this change.[1]

Tension in The Hague

Leading AK Party politicians arranged a conference on equality in Turkey, 'honour' killings and violence against women in The Hague in November 2004. The atmosphere was tense. Only two days earlier, the Dutch film director Theo van Gogh had been brutally murdered by a radical Islamist, shortly after his highly controversial film *Submission*, on the abuse of Muslim women, was broadcast on national television in the Netherlands. Security concerns were on everyone's mind. The mistrust between the West and Islam felt almost tangible as the weekend conference was opened on an early Saturday morning while rain was pouring down outside the hotel in the Dutch capital.

Ayşe Böhürler, an AK Party board executive and well-known media personality, surprised with her opening speech by frankly describing the resistance within the governing party towards arranging this series of conferences in EU capitals on violence against women. 'Why expose our domestic problems in EU countries?' was the argument of those opposing the idea. But the unreserved support to go ahead from

1. KA-MER 2004 Report, *No More 'if onlys'. Killings in the Name of Honour*, (in Turkish/English).

Prime Minister Erdoğan and the then Foreign Minister Gül secured the sequences of conferences, described Mrs Böhürler, who was one of the founding members of the AK Party. By wearing a headscarf, she was automatically disqualified from becoming a member of parliament.

Agreement existed at the conference that violence against women and girls occurs in every segment of society, regardless of country, class, culture and ethnicity. Statistics presented by the UN showed that one in three women throughout the world will suffer from violence during her lifetime. In EU countries the same figure is one in five.[1] The need to protect an individual's rights rather than the family's rights was emphasized by some speakers as essential to achieve progress. Forty per cent of Turkish women tolerated that their husbands beat them, according to a study carried out by a Turkish university.[2] Accepting violence was viewed as a way of protecting the family. There are a growing number of campaigns in Turkey to prevent violence against women. All army conscripts for example are briefed on the subject as part of their curriculum.

Parliamentary findings on 'honour' killings

Besides the government, Parliament also worked actively on human rights for women. Broad consensus existed on the need for comprehensive action. A parliamentary commission investigated 'honour' killings, describing a number of abusive acts and domestic torture committed against women in its 292-page report, which was presented in February 2006. Locked up at home, having ears and noses cut off and being forced to commit suicide were some acts listed in the report. The Commission recommended a simplified judicial system in favour of the victim and institutionalized methods offering assistance

---

1.   Address at the conference by Anne-Birgitte Albrectsen, UNFPA Representative for Turkey.
2.   Hacettepe University (Ankara), Demographics and Health Survey 2003, presented in August 2004.

to abused girls. Educational programmes should be launched aiming to change male mindsets, and seminars for members of the judiciary, police, teachers and social workers on violence perpetrated against women and children were some of the recommendations in the detailed report. More shelters and safe houses were also called for.

Headscarves: A women's rights issue?

She was an assertive and attractive Turkish woman in her late twenties, who had two university degrees as well as plenty of frustration. 'Why should I accept being discriminated against?' she asked me rhetorically during a break at a conference on Turkish–EU relations, which we both attended in Ankara. Wearing a headscarf stopped her from pursuing her dreams of an academic career in Turkey and had obliged her to study abroad. Her hopes that the AK government would manage to abolish the headscarf ban in state institutions were waning after three years.

The headscarf ban has been gradually implemented since 1998. Until then, a certain pragmatism prevailed and headscarves could be seen worn on campuses and by government employees. When the Constitutional Court decided to close down the Islamic 'Welfare Party', which ran the country until it was forced to resign in 1997, it also mentioned in its decision that the scarf should be banned at universities. This practice was soon applied to civil servants too.

Wearing a headscarf is increasingly debated as a human rights issue by those struggling for 'headscarf freedom'. Although some girls, in the meantime, choose to circumvent the dress code at schools and universities by an unusual method; they put a wig on top of their headscarves. Among these are daughters of cabinet ministers. Increasingly, the argument is made that it concerns not only freedom of religion and the right to education but also women's rights. That, however, implies that a girl or young woman is given a choice whether or not to wear a Muslim headscarf, rather than having it imposed by a family member or relative.

When the European Court of Human Rights (ECHR) adopted the same view on the Islamic headscarf ban as the Turkish Constitutional Court, there was great disappointment among those opposing the restrictions. In a landmark decision in 2004, the ECHR unanimously ruled that Leyla Şahin, a medical student wearing an Islamic headscarf, had not had her human rights violated when she was forced to discontinue her studies in Istanbul in 1998.[1]

An appeal to a higher court of the ECHR was rejected in late 2005, resulting in disillusion among the AK Party and many of its religious grass-roots supporters. Their hopes were dashed that European institutions such as the EU or the Council of Europe could resolve the issue, which the government party hitherto had been unable to do, despite an overwhelming majority in Parliament. Opposition from powerful secular institutions such as the judiciary, bureaucracy and the military was simply too strong.

The EU has not commented on the issue in its annual Progress Reports on Turkey over the years. The senior EU politician Joost Lagendijk, on the other hand, has for some time been advocating that university students should be allowed to wear headscarves. The outspoken Mr Lagendijk, a staunch supporter of Turkey's EU bid, has a high profile in Turkey as the co-chairman of the Turkey–EU joint parliamentarian commission. He is often quoted on front pages in the Turkish press.

The debate on the Islamic headscarf shows no signs of abating. It evokes strong emotions on both sides. Some easing-off of the restrictions is probable in the future but only after the political climate has calmed down, especially after the twin elections in 2007 when the headscarf became the symbol of the deeply diverging views on the place of religion in the Turkish society.

---

1.   ECHR decision, 29 June 2004, application no. 44774/98.

Far-reaching new legislation

Turkey's EU reform process brought significant legal improvements to women's rights. It started with the new Civil Code, which was adopted by Parliament in autumn 2001, resulting in men and women becoming equals within the family for the first time. When the concept of the head of the family was abolished, permission from a husband before a wife took a job was no longer necessary. Goods acquired during a marriage would by law be shared on an equal basis, although its implementation has been very limited, noted the EU in its Progress Report a few years later.

The Civil Code, which entered into force in January 2002, was generally very well received. One secular academic from Ankara, though, whom I met at a buffet dinner hosted by an EU colleague, was unhappy. He worried it would lead to 'having board meetings at the kitchen table from now on.'

The Constitution was amended in 2004,[1] giving supremacy to international conventions on basic rights and freedoms over all national legislation. The UN Convention on the Elimination of All Forms of Discrimination Against Women (CEDAW)[2] is one of the international instruments to which the Turkish state is party.

A new, progressive Penal Code was introduced in 2004, which addressed several key women's rights issues. Violence against women became an offence against the individual, not the family or society. Life imprisonment was envisaged for killings motivated by 'tradition and customs', a rule intending to address the 'honour' killings. Virginity tests would lead to imprisonment unless there was a court order. Sexual assault within marriage was criminalized, unlike in some existing EU countries. A perpetrator of rape could no longer escape

---

1.   Article 40, in May 2004.
2.   CEDAW was signed by Turkey in 1985 and ratified in 1986 with certain reservations, which were withdrawn in 1999 when the Civil Code was reviewed. The Optional Protocol to the Convention was signed in 2000 and ratified in 2002.

punishment by marrying his victim. Polygamy would result in slightly increased prison sentences.

Overall, the Penal Code was met with praise, including from women's rights organizations in Turkey, who had successfully lobbied for the new legislation for several years. The well-coordinated campaign by around fifty women's NGOs vis-à-vis the Turkish government, Parliament and the EU Commission and EU embassies in Ankara resulted in thirty of their thirty-five proposals being met.

Genuine transformation for women?

When I first arrived as a diplomat to Turkey in 2001, women's rights seemed marginalized. It was seldom a topic of discussion among politicians, diplomats or civil society. But remarkable changes were to take place during the following years. A strong political determination to make progress in the EU bid and to enhance respect for human rights by complying with EU standards paved the way for substantial legal reforms. An increasingly active and efficient women's movement became an instrumental part of that process. Turkish media contributed largely by paying close attention, particularly to 'honour' killings and girls' school attendance. The largest newspaper, *Hürriyet*, launched its own two-year awareness campaign on violence against women, using buses up and down the country to promote the cause. The newspaper *Milliyet* initiated a similar campaign: 'Daddy, send me to school'. Both newspapers are headed by female members of the owners – the Doğan family.

Today's Turkey is still struggling with women's rights although far-reaching improvements have been achieved. The EU reform process propelled new, key legislation but violence against women remains a persistent and widespread problem. The high rate of illiteracy and noticeably low level of women's participation in politics are other protracted problems, which means that Atatürk's revolution of reforms partly remains unfinished.

Prime Minister Erdoğan and his government often stressed that reforms are carried out to benefit Turkey's own citizens as well as fulfilling EU conditions. The implementation of the amendments and new legislation will be crucial. If the positive transformation of women's rights carries on, it would allow both men and women to fully develop their potential, which would contribute to the development and prosperity of Turkey. In addition, respect for women's rights will make an important impact on EU public opinion towards Turkey as the membership process unfolds.

Contrasting images

'I cannot believe this is Turkey. It is like another world.' Those were comments made by a Turkish female friend of mine, who read this chapter (when it was still only a draft) while we were on a private boat cruise along part of Turkey's rugged and unspoiled Aegean coast. We were three families, all with different religions; Muslim, Christian and Jewish. It was in late August 2006 and the temperature lingered around forty degrees, the hottest days in twenty years, and forest fires were ravaging the coast. As we discussed the situation of women in Turkey, watching the smoke of the fires, the final home of Virgin Mary, mother of Jesus, was rescued just before the fire reached the tiny stone building, which is now a shrine. We all found it miraculous. Mary (or Maryam) is highly regarded by Muslims and she is the only woman directly mentioned in the Qur'an.[1]

My friend felt that modern Turkish women like herself, were overlooked in this chapter. She, being a successful entrepreneur from Istanbul, married and a mother of two, felt that the image portrayed of Turkish women was too gloomy and limited. I agreed with her. The focus is on 'the other'; many of them women of Kurdish origin, whose lifestyle and conditions are so different – and unknown – to most Europeans.

Career women in Turkey are leading similar lives to their successful

---

1.   Mary is mentioned several times in the Qur'an, in particular in the Sourate 19, as a virgin and the mother of the Prophet Jesus.

Western European counterparts. The contrast, though, with women living in poverty- stricken parts of Turkey is conspicuously different and unfamiliar. When I first visited Diyarbakir in 2002 I arrived late on a cold winter evening. A few women's organizations had asked to meet me. To my surprise, around ten Kurdish women, young and old, were waiting for me although it was after ten in the evening, all wrapped up in layers of clothes in the sparsely heated hotel lobby. They told me about their plight of not being able to read or write, arranged marriages at an early age and their very few choices in life. Despite all the hardship, the women were not dejected. Their hope for the future was tied up with the Turkish EU membership, trusting that that would bring them human rights. Their belief in the EU as a catalyst for change in their harsh lives was touching and left a deep impression on me.

EIGHT

Changing US–Turkish Relations and their Impact on the EU Process

It was the day of the 9/11 terror attacks against the US. My first week in Turkey was about to end with another round of courtesy visits to foreign ambassadors, this time to the German ambassador. On the way I learnt from my driver about the first wave of attacks in New York. At the hotel in Ankara, where I was staying with my family waiting for our goods and pets to arrive from Lebanon, a subdued atmosphere prevailed. We were only a handful of guests staying at the Sheraton, reflecting the severe economic crisis which had hit Turkey earlier that year. The other guests were mainly American businessmen, who were now quietly speculating on the shocking events and how many days it would be before they would be able to fly home. I was relieved that my young daughter, who is American as well as Swedish, had not been alone in the hotel room watching the second attack on the World Trade Center live on television, but together with her father.

I flew to Istanbul the following day, and morning was breaking at the large, international hotel in the city where I was checking in. The lobby was full of stranded American tourists. With transatlantic flights cancelled for an indeterminate length of time, they were all unable to return home. A burly Texan, standing next to me, pointed to a Saudi Arabian woman walking by the reception desk, completely covered in a black veil and cloak. 'How do we know she is not a terrorist?' he screamed. Being stranded in a Muslim country seemed to fuel his fear. Most of the tourists were calm but a few were clearly bewildered.

Meanwhile, a friend and key figure in Lebanese politics called me from Beirut. He had almost lost his voice while endlessly trying to convince the Americans that Lebanon and Hezbollah had nothing to do with the terror attacks. He predicted that we – both the Muslim world and the West – were facing a very difficult future.

Only hours after the 9/11 terror attacks, the Turkish prime minister, Ecevit, expressed his unqualified support for America's response, thus becoming the first leader of a Muslim country to do so. The Turkish prime minister later volunteered to send Turkish soldiers to Afghanistan despite opinion polls showing significant opposition.

Twice a year, the US and EU ambassadors had meetings in Ankara. At one such lunch meeting the well-liked US ambassador Bob Pearson briefed us about the US-led war on terror. Turkey needed only fifteen minutes of this before giving the go-ahead to the US government to use its airspace and Incirlik, an airbase in southern Turkey located 2,400 kilometres away from Afghanistan. Turkey later took command of the International Security and Assistance Force (ISAF) in Afghanistan.

The financial meltdown in Turkey in early 2001, followed by the US-supported IMF recovery programmes for Turkey and the attacks in New York and Washington, meant that both countries had been through nightmare events. Their strategic partnership provided welcome support when help was most needed, as the former US ambassador to Turkey, Mark Parris, summed up in an article.[1] However, the US–Turkish strategic partnership was soon to undergo

---

1.　Mark Parris, 'Starting Over: US–Turkish Relations in the Post-Iraq War Era', Turkish Policy Quarterly, vol. 2, no. 1, spring 2003.

a major shift, which also had implications for Turkey's image in the EU as a potential American Trojan horse.

Turkey had been in the orbit of American power and influence for decades. The war in Iraq changed that, causing an unexpected watershed in US–Turkish relations. The question arose whether relations between the US and Turkey would ever become as important again as they used to be. But it was not the first time that that question had been asked. US relations with its long-time ally and friend Turkey had been through turbulent times before. Meanwhile, the accelerated EU process of recent years offered Turkey a potentially new strategic position.

From close military ally to strategic partner

When the Truman Doctrine was launched in March 1947, it marked the official US acknowledgment of the cold war. US military and economic aid was provided to Turkey and Greece, to stop them from falling to communism. Since the implementation of the Truman Doctrine in the summer of 1947, US loans and grants have amounted to 12.5 billion dollars in economic aid and 14 billion dollars in military assistance to Turkey.[1]

Shared values and ideas on regional and global objectives brought American and Turkish soldiers together in many battlefields, from Korea to, more recently, Kosovo and Kabul, to name but a few. In Korea they were fighting shoulder to shoulder under the UN flag against the North Koreans, who were advised and equipped by the Soviets. This is not a forgotten historical event but very much part of the Turkish collective memory. The collaboration with the US in Korea more than half a century ago was often brought up by Turks in conversations I had on US–Turkish relations, especially during 2003, when bilateral relations were seriously strained. History is kept alive in Turkey in a way dissimilar to or rarely shown in the US or

---

1.   US Department of State, Bureau of Europe and Eurasia Affairs, April 2006.

in Western European countries. To serve at the embassy in Seoul is traditionally viewed by Turkish diplomats as a gratifying task thanks to the common war history.

The collaboration in Korea paved the way for Turkey's NATO membership in 1952, making Turkey a trusted ally and solid bulwark against the Soviet Union. Turkey's NATO membership was also a logical culmination of the Truman Doctrine. Thus the Alliance's southeastern flank was protected and strengthened against communism by a country which had the additional benefit of being a democratic, secular state in a Muslim society and with a market economy. This was part of the cold war strategy of creating a 'northern tier' of nations to contain the spread of Soviet power into the Middle East. The tier consisted of Greece, Turkey, Iran and Pakistan.

Once Turkey had taken the step from neutrality to becoming a staunch ally of the US and the West in the 1940s, relations between Ankara and Washington were dominated by defence and security matters. The military-to-military relations were close and strong. As the cold war came to an end, the new strategic role of Turkey was far from obvious.

Turkey did not take on a leading, regional role in the Caucasus and Central Asia as was initially anticipated. Turkish President Özal articulated in 1991–1992 a desire for Turkey to assert leadership among Turkic-speaking people in those regions. Given the prevalence of Wahhabism money and jihadist influence in the Caucasus and Central Asia, it might have been beneficial had Turkey played a bigger role there during the 1990s.

Instead, it was the first Gulf War, starting with Iraq's invasion of Kuwait, which redefined Turkey's role in global politics. By supporting the Allied invasion of Iraq in early 1991 and participating in the Iraqi oil embargo, Turkey positioned itself as a strategic ally in the post-cold-war era. Turkish participation with peacekeeping forces in the Balkans, East Africa and the Middle East underlined Ankara's willingness and capability as a military partner. The use of the military base Incirlik in southern Turkey for US and British aircrafts to patrol the 'no-fly zone' in northern Iraq during the 1990s illustrated the new level of US–Turkish cooperation. It culminated in Turkey being declared a 'strategic partner' by President Clinton during his cheered official visit to Turkey in 1999. That term was traditionally saved for exceptionally close allies, such as Israel. US–Turkish relations had reached a new and profound maturity. Another important factor was the Turkish role in NATO. The Turkish peacekeepers involved in the NATO-led Implementation Force (IFOR) in Bosnia and Hercegovina in the mid-1990s, which was later followed by the Stabilization Force (SFOR) and Turkish participation in the Kosovo Force (KFOR) launched in 1999, were also important to forging the strategic partnership, as was Turkey's importance as an energy hub.

The Turkish–Israeli strategic relationship, which underpinned the Oslo peace process, was another feature contributing to prosperous US–Turkish relations at the time. The close position that the US and Turkey held with regard to the European Defense and Security Policy (ESDP), a major element of the EU's common foreign policy and security policy, and EU relations to NATO military assets were other factors. Furthermore, US–Turkish relations in the late 1990s were much more aligned with regard to Syria and Iran.

The long-standing geo-strategic partnership and close relations between the Pentagon and the Turkish armed forces reflected onto political matters. The four military interventions and coups in Ankara over the years (1961, 1971, 1980 and 1997) resulted in muted opposition, if any, in Washington compared with that in many European capitals.

Although close strategic and military objectives dominated US–Turkish relations during four decades, two issues created recurring strains; Cyprus and the Armenian question. Both are major hurdles in Turkey's EU process.

Cyprus and the 'Johnson letter'

When intercommunal violence erupted in Cyprus on Christmas Eve 1963, started by attacks against Turks, President Lyndon Johnson warned the Turkish government not to intervene in a letter signed by him, which was drafted by the Under-Secretary of State, George Ball. NATO would not be bound to assist Turkey if the Soviet Union were to become involved in the conflict, Johnson stated in his often-quoted letter. It was viewed as an unfair veto against Turkish affairs and had a long-lasting, negative effect on Turkish people's attitudes towards the US. It caused a crisis at the time, but this passed and relations still remained close.

The 'Johnson letter' is still occasionally referred to, more than forty years later, in discussions on Cyprus in Ankara. For me, it was an unfamiliar concept despite my intensive reading on Turkish politics before taking up my new post. Studies before moving to a new country have a remarkable tendency to act as fluid knowledge, however, once one is settled in, facts and history stick like super-glue to one's memory. Most of my ambassadorial colleagues in Ankara learnt about their new posting only some months in advance, like me, leaving little time for any extensive preparations. The US and British ambassadors were usually exceptions in knowing up to a year beforehand where they would move to next and this was often reflected in their language skills.

In 1974, the Cyprus issue caused yet another crisis in US–Turkish relations although this time around it was more prolonged. After a coup by the Greek Cypriots, Turkish armed forces moved into Cyprus in July 1974, dividing the island. This initial incursion was met with some sympathy by the Nixon administration. The difficulties came after the second Turkish incursion, almost four weeks later, on 15 August 1974. US Congress voted for an arms embargo against Turkey. The retaliatory action consisted of closing down most of the American military bases in Turkey. Subsequently, President Carter took action, which eventually resulted in a lifting of the four-year-old embargo.

Turkey returned to its position as the key flank country in Western defence towards the Soviet Union. The US position on Cyprus from then on focused to a large extent on avoiding Greek–Turkish tensions so as not to threaten unity within NATO. With improving Greek–Turkish relations, beginning in 1999, Cyprus became less of a US security concern while diplomatic efforts were stepped up to find a solution. Increasingly, these were carried out in close coordination with the UN and the EU.

EU accession a catalyst for change on Cyprus

The Bush administration and the European Union saw the period 1999–2004 as an opportunity to solve the long-standing Cyprus problem. The island's scheduled EU accession in spring 2004, with or without a settlement, and Turkey's strong commitment to be able to start membership negotiations, created an unprecedented opportunity. Prime Minister Erdoğan's surprising and bold initiatives to find a way forward from early 2003 onwards impressed Washington and Brussels. However, there was severe US disappointment when Ankara allowed the Turkish Cypriot leader Rauf Denktaş to undermine the Hague round of talks on the UN 'Annan Plan' in March 2003. Prime Minister Erdoğan managed to skilfully handle domestic opposition among elements of the powerful military and in the Turkish Foreign Ministry, which still insisted on independence and sovereignty for the 'Turkish Republic of Northern Cyprus'. But it was only after the change of government policy on Northern Cyprus in 2004, led by 'Prime Minister' Talat,[1] who was committed to the reunification of Cyprus, that President Bush concluded it was worth putting some diplomatic capital into the peace efforts, which Colin Powell did with gusto.

'Turkey's most popular politician', was a frequently used epithet for

---

1. Mehmet Ali Talat became 'Prime Minister' after an election in April 2005. Since Northern Cyprus is not internationally recognized, his political positions are within inverted commas.

the Turkish Cypriot leader Denktaş, which started to lose its validity as painstaking progress was made towards peace and reunification of the island in the 'Annan Plan'. Named after the UN Secretary-General, the plan was drawn up by the UN, the US and the EU. Rauf Denktaş frequently visited Turkey. One of his arrivals in Ankara turned into a measure of the support for his policy on Cyprus. The supporters of the Turkish Cypriot leader were encouraged to greet him *en masse* at Esenboğa airport. Rumours were rife in political circles in Ankara that it would turn into a massive demonstration against the government's new policy on Cyprus. In the end, few turned up at the airport, almost an hour's drive north of the city centre.

The Turkish Cypriots' approval of the 'Annan Plan' to reunite the island in the 2004 referendum, while rejected by the Greek Cypriots, was a huge blow to the government in Ankara. The government had taken a considerable political risk on the home front with its vigorous and brave campaign to contribute to a solution of the Cyprus problem. The Turkish government's role as a constructive Cyprus negotiator, leaving its international image as a spoiler behind, resulted in abundant goodwill from the US and the EU. But Turkey expected – and deserved – more. Despite substantial new assistance from the US, a perceived lack of concrete international action to improve the situation for the Turkish Cypriots caused widespread resentment in Turkey. This created a fertile environment for nationalists, who were at the starting blocks to regain ground lost since the general election in 2002.

After the failure of the spring referendum in 2004, US policy on Cyprus moved its focus to easing the economic isolation of the Turkish Cypriots and assisting with institution building. US political efforts to find a solution were scaled down, as there were no signs of change by the Greek Cypriots. The Greek Cypriot leader Papadopoulos deserved the 'Yasser Arafat Award – For Turning Down a Good Deal,' commented one disenchanted US official.

Meanwhile, the Turkish EU accession talks were threatened by a lack of agreement on allowing Greek Cypriot aircraft and vessels into Turkish ports and harbours. While the EU Commissioner for Enlargement, Ollie Rehn, warned of a 'a train crash' and suspended negotiations in autumn 2006 if the ports were not opened up, Prime Minister Erdoğan was determined not to give in until the isolation of the Turkish Cypriots was eased. '700,000 Greek Cypriots' interests stand against those of seventy million Turks,' was an argument often used by the Turkish leader.

The deadlock on the Cyprus question led to a decision by the EU leaders in December 2006 to bring in restrictions on Turkey's membership talks.

The Armenian question

It was 24 April 2005 and the ninetieth year of commemorating the alleged Armenian genocide, which was vehemently rejected by Turkey. BBC News was showing a lengthy documentary film of the mass killings of Armenians during the tail end of the Ottoman Empire. I was alone watching the programme on the new flat-screen TV in the VIP lounge at the airport in Ankara, wary that someone else might come into the lounge. The question was so controversial and emotional in Turkey that I knew I was risking a scene if another passenger came into the lounge. It was with a sigh of relief that I finished watching it before any other VIP passengers started to arrive. After almost four years in Turkey, I was acutely aware of the dynamite constituted by the Armenian issue, despite recent attempts by the government to defuse it by having historians from both sides discuss it.

It brought back memories of a visitor who came to see me when I was in charge of human rights at the Swedish UN mission in Geneva in the late 1990s. The visitor was a painfully frail and stooped man in his late eighties with a story to tell. He was a survivor of what he described as the Armenian genocide, when up to 1.5 million people were killed, eager to share his story before it was too late. Most of the other survivors had already passed away. We were meeting in my bland, impersonal office, compensated by a beautiful lake view. In that setting, the tiny old man quietly briefed me about his horrifying experiences as a ten-year-old boy, before leaving for his next meeting at another diplomatic mission, busy preparing for the annual session of the UN Commission on Human Rights.

In Ankara, I often encountered the Turkish version of the tragic events, always stirring passionate emotions, sometimes aggressively defensive. It was yet another example of history being alive and very much part of current affairs. Ninety years on, the Armenian issue still plays a delicate and controversial role in US–Turkish relations. While recognizing the mass killings of Armenians as genocide is not part of EU conditions or the Copenhagen Criteria, it still plays a role in Turkey's EU bid. The emphasis is on the curbing of freedom of expression in Turkey, notoriously symbolized by the novelist and Nobel Prize winner Orhan Pamuk's ordeals. To these were added the case of Elif Şafak, another author who faced prosecution for insulting the Turkish state according to the controversial Article 301 of the Turkish criminal code.

The frequently used idiom 'A Turk's only friend is another Turk' illustrates the sentiments of being unfairly treated and cornered by the US and European countries on the Armenian issue. Every spring, annual attempts are made in US Congress to have a resolution adopted recognizing the genocide. For several years, active lobbying by President George W. Bush prevented it from being passed. The Jewish lobby in Washington also contributed to stopping the resolution from being passed. Those efforts are a reflection of Turkey's uniquely close relations with Israel. Despite fierce lobbying of President Bush, a non-binding resolution was approved in October 2007 by a committee in the US House of Representative, labelling the massacres as genocide. The chairman of the foreign affairs committee was himself a survivor of the Holocaust. The measure sparked off an intense controversy between the two NATO allies. It only subsided a few weeks later when the resolution was not taken for a vote in the full House of Representatives but put on the back burner.

Failure to open the Turkish border to Armenia has also resulted in US criticism. On the Turkish side, the Armenian issue includes frustration and dissatisfaction at the often forgotten Armenian occupation of Azeri territory, resulting in large numbers of internally displaced people. The killing of more than thirty Turkish diplomats by Armenian terrorists between 1973 and 1994 is another source of frustration over the feeling that Turkish sufferings are not being properly accounted for by the international community.

The impact of the Armenian diaspora in the US and elsewhere should not be overlooked. In France, where the Armenians number around 400,000, it was acutely felt in October 2006, when the French National Assembly passed a law that criminalized the denial of the Armenian genocide by the Ottoman Empire in the early twentieth century. Turkey was in uproar. Demonstrations followed against the French embassy in Ankara, where a black wreath was left outside by angry demonstrators.

However, there have been promising steps taken in Turkish–Armenian relations. Direct talks between foreign minister Abdullah Gül and his Armenian counterpart, launched in summer 2003, and direct flights between Istanbul and Yerevan were signs of progress towards improved relations. During regular meetings between the Turkish foreign minister and EU ambassadors in Ankara, on matters apart from EU-related issues, the attempts to normalize Turkey's relations with Armenia were often mentioned. Clearly, this was an area where Abdullah Gül wanted to see some movement. It remains to be seen what he can and would like to achieve in his new role as president.

Iraq created a watershed

As the US government intensified its preparations for an invasion of Iraq in early 2003, the political temperature in Ankara was reaching fever pitch. Slow progress was made during the months of US–Turkish negotiations, which were becoming increasingly antagonistic. Permission to have US troops based and in transit in Turkey and the use of Turkish airbases was sluggish to materialize. The Speaker of Parliament, Bülent Arinç, was the only AK Party heavyweight taking an open stand against allowing US troops into Turkey. Arinç, a lawyer in his mid-fifties, had his base among religiously conservative AK Party circles, described by some as fundamentalists, who were estimated to make up around 8 per cent of the party's supporters.

Following the appointment of Bülent Arinç as Speaker, after robust positioning by himself, ambassadors had requested individual courtesy calls to see him in accordance with well-established diplomatic tradition. However, with crucial decisions coming up in Parliament the Speaker had let it be known, understandably, that for the time being he was unable to receive foreign ambassadors. Therefore, I was pleasantly surprised when I learnt I would see him only a day after my request. I believe an exception was made for me as the only female ambassador among the EU member states in Turkey, to refute rumours that for religious reasons he resented dealing with women. Our meeting turned out to be in late February 2003, just days before a parliamentary vote which would shake the foundation of US–Turkish relations.

As an invasion of Iraq was drawing closer, the newly elected Turkish government gave the green light to 62,000 American soldiers being posted in and transiting through the country during a six-month period. But the controversial decision, delayed several times, needed approval by Parliament. During my meeting with the Speaker, he reflected in his serene but resolute way that 'Parliament is facing a difficult decision. The Turkish population does not want a war in Iraq,' while being vague about the likely outcome of the imminent voting. 'Everything is possible,' he said.

On 1 March 2003, the day of the voting, 45,000 people demonstrated on the streets of Ankara against a war. Meanwhile, the

Turkish military took an atypical position by abstaining from publicly expressing its opinion. The lack of a firm and favourable position towards its close military ally was generally believed to have worked against US interests. The Turkish army was the most respected institution among the population, and its opinion mattered. The major opposition party, the CHP, traditionally close to the military, was openly against allowing US troops to transit. The silver lining of a six billion US dollar grant that could have been leveraged into twenty-four billion in low cost loans and the right for Turkish troops to enter northern Iraq with the Americans did not seem to diminish the strong opposition. If there had been an agreement, both the US and Turkey would have had forces in northern Iraq to deal with the PKK problem there, which has bedevilled their relationship ever since. Two months of bilateral negotiations were coming to an end. It was now up to Parliament to make the final decision.

When Parliament unpredictably rejected the US government's request, with only a minimum margin, shock waves reverberated through the US–Turkish strategic partnership. The motion failed because it fell four votes short of an absolute majority of those present and voting, due to the high number of abstentions. Outwardly, relations remained firm. The formal US reaction was a restrained acceptance of the stunning outcome: 'Turkey is a democracy,' was a frequently heard comment. The provisional AK government,[1] waiting for its leader Erdoğan to be allowed to take office as prime minister, felt it had genuinely done what it could to pass the motion by Parliament.

The overwhelming majority of the members of parliament were newcomers to national politics and were besieged by phone calls, letters and faxes from their constituencies appealing for a 'no-vote'. Many I spoke to later felt that they simply had no other choice than

---

1. The Abdullah Gül-led government resigned on 11 March 2003 after 113 days in power, to enable Tayyip Erdoğan to take over as prime minister, as was expected once his ban on holding public office had been cleared.

to vote against. They also felt unclear about what exactly the military agreement with the US contained. Opinion polls the day before the crucial parliamentary vote showed 95 per cent of the population was against a war in Iraq. Despite all these factors, there was still a general expectation that Tayyip Erdoğan, from his strong position as party leader, would be able to deliver just enough yes-votes from the AK parliamentarians. This was in contrast to the parliamentary vote in October 2003 on the motion to send Turkish divisions to Iraq to become part of the stabilization force. In that case Prime Minister Erdoğan had a public vote, he sat in the hall as votes were cast and passed the motion overwhelmingly despite roughly the same level of public opposition. In the end, the top US official Paul Bremer, who governed Iraq for fourteen months after the invasion, failed to get the Iraqis to agree to the Turkish deployment.

Turkey's failure to approve the Bush administration's request undercut the previously tight allied relationship in an unprecedented way. Neither the Cyprus crisis in the 1970s, nor the much-criticized poppy growing in Turkey around the same time, could compare to the intensity of the mutual disappointment and distrust it created. When the Turkish government three weeks later, in late March 2003, offered its full cooperation, it was too late. Alternative invasion plans were already set by the US. A slew of strong feelings on both sides resulted, which still lingered several years later. The US government held the state institutions to blame rather than the AK Party. Over time, however, that has changed. Today, relations between the US and military and state institutions such as the Ministry of Foreign Affairs and the National Intelligence Agency, MIT,[1] are better than with the government, according to a top official in Washington.

Initially, it was bilateral military relations that suffered. Washington blamed the Turkish state for the failure, not the AK government. In particular, the Kemalist establishment, among them the military, was held responsible. Together with the main opposition party, the

---

1.   *Milli Istihbarat Teskilati* (MIT).

CHP, traditionally close to the military establishment, their actions were viewed by many observers as an attempt to undermine the AK government. Domestically, the inexperienced government could be blamed either way: for damaging US–Turkish relations in the case of a failure to pass the motion in Parliament or – in the case of a 'yes' vote – for allowing the US troops' passage despite huge opposition among the population.

But with the Iraqi war dragging on, political relations between the Bush and Erdoğan governments gradually started to be negatively affected. The US lack of priority in addressing the PKK/Kongra-Gel terrorists and their bases in northern Iraq acted like an abscess within Turkey, consuming bilateral relations. The disunity on how to deal with the PKK and which policy to pursue in the Middle East were major stumbling blocks to a return to close and smooth relations. The strategic partnership, as visualized by its architects, had de facto been downgraded to a strategic alliance after only a few years. Some would obviously dispute this, while the range of internal opinions held by the US government tells its own tale.

EU considerations for Turkey in the Iraq War

There were several considerations for Turkey regarding its conduct during the Iraq War. Before war broke out, there was anxiety about how Turkey would deal with a humanitarian crisis, with potentially huge numbers of Iraqi refugees crossing the 200-kilometre mountainous border with Turkey. Considering that the PKK's bases were in northern Iraq, leading to insurgency and terrorist attacks in Turkey, there were fears that in a worst-case scenario, the Turkish–Iraqi borders would be closed for security reasons to refugees trying to flee Saddam Hussein's forces.[1]

---

1. The Turkish military presence, with 1,500 men and weapons to fight the PKK in northern Iraq, was acknowledged by the then chief of staff, General Özkök, in a rare interview with the newspaper *Radical*, summarized in the *Turkish Daily News*, 10 November 2003.

The major concern, though, was the fear of excessive violence against Kurds in northern Iraq if Turkish troops went in. Such an outcome would cause a serious setback, if not complete stalling, of the promising Turkish EU process.

The Iraq War exposed a fault line in foreign policy within the EU, the first to make itself known. Its effects rippled all the way into EU meetings in Ankara, making discussions more muted than usual. When France and Germany took a diametrically opposite position in response to the US-led invasion than the UK, Italy and several soon-to-be-EU members in Eastern Europe, the two sides of the divide were labelled 'old and new Europe' by US Secretary of Defense Donald Rumsfeld. Turkey did not easily fit into either of these two categorizations of Europe, nor were there any attempts to make it do so. Multi-faceted Turkey was too unique for an easy label.

The rift within the EU was misread by many in Turkey. Turkey's rejection of the US proposal on troop transfers had a surprising number of Turkish politicians and some analysts believing it would benefit Turkey's EU process and create general goodwill. Many thought that the outcome of the 1 March vote in Parliament illustrated 'democracy at work' as well as support of the French–German position. This was a miscalculation, at least in the short term. The EU was too preoccupied with its own damaging division to pay much attention. The Turkish position might be helpful, though, in the longer-term perspective, by undermining any argument that Turkey would become an American Trojan horse once inside the EU. Sceptics of Turkish EU membership on those grounds suddenly found they had a weakened case.

While passionate debates raged about the Turkish position on the Iraq War, I could not help but be personally concerned about a more mundane question. Rumours were circulating that the excellent American school in Ankara, run by the US Department of Defense, and attended by my daughter, would have to close down shortly. Fears that in the future too few American children would enrol threatened its existence. With no US troops launched from Turkey into Iraq and strategic importance appearing to shift eastwards, beyond Turkey, things looked gloomy for the school. Luckily (with exceptionally few choices for foreign children in Ankara), the small school remained open. Its website, showing a tall teenager tenderly holding hands with a tiny pre-school child, which my daughter and I had seen while checking out the options before moving to Ankara, had convinced us. It was the friendly image that we both liked.

Several incidents in the Iraq War further damaged US–Turkish relations. Eleven Turkish Special Forces soldiers were captured and hooded by Americans in Suleymaniya, which caused an outcry and injured national pride in Turkey. The 'Suleymaniya incident' in the Kurdish region of Iraq[1] on 4 July 2003 is likely to be remembered and referred to for years to come by the Turks. US–Turkish relations were further eroded when top AK Party politicians in November 2004 described the second US battle against insurgency in Fallujah as genocide. Turkey's 'unacceptable overreaction' was put down to Sunni solidarity, one US official in Ankara mentioned in private.

The Turkish blockbuster movie *Valley of the Wolves – Iraq* opened in early 2006 and further chilled US–Turkish relations. Most Europeans have never heard of the movie, but it quickly gained notoriety and rekindled resentment in political circles in Washington. The graphic film, sometimes described as a Turkish revenge on *Midnight Express*, was highly anti-American and anti-Semitic as well as having anti-Christian undertones. In spring 2006, the skilful deputy AK Party leader Şaban Dişli tried to mend fences with the US administration during a trip to Washington together with Mr Zapsu, another close adviser of the prime minister. Both sides faced a tough, uphill battle.

US–Turkish relations were poisoned by the increasing PKK attacks against Turkey from bases in northern Iraq. In Turkey, the perception deepened that the US sided with the Kurds in Iraq at the expense of

---

1.   The Kurdistan region as referred to in the Iraqi Constitution of 2005, section 5: Powers of the Region, chapter 1: Regions.

Turkish security concerns. A summit in the White House in autumn 2007 mitigated those concerns, at least for a time. When Turkish aircraft bombed PKK targets deep inside northern Iraq, followed by an incursion of several hundred Turkish troops in December 2007, there were rumours of a tacit agreement between Turkey and the US.

In Turkey, increasing resentment of American policy in the Middle East translated into antagonism towards the US as a whole. Opinion polls showed approval ratings for the US falling in many countries, Turkey included, as the Iraq War continued.[1] The strategic partnership announced by President Clinton in the Turkish Parliament in 1999 seemed a long way away.

Shift in Turkish foreign policy

Since the late 1990s Turkey's foreign relations experienced major changes in terms of trends and dynamics, facilitated by and linked to the EU integration process. Gone was the cold war era, which had contributed a certain amount of predictability and order. While Turkey's role in US foreign policy grew, not least in economic terms, Turkey was simultaneously pursuing EU membership. The Customs Union with the EU and securing Turkey's status as an EU candidate country were illustrious examples of success after decades of setbacks.

New trends in the decision-making process

The new millennium, though, brought the blossoming relations between the US and Turkey to a surprising low point in 2003, and gradually turned it into a crisis. US–Turkish cooperation could no longer be taken for granted. Actions leading up to the rejection of passage for US forces to northern Iraq through Turkey highlighted a new phenomenon; the decision-making process had changed. Up till then it had been widely assumed that the Turkish military had the

---

1.　Pew Research Center's poll in March 2004 found that unfavourable views of the US outnumbered favourable views by 63 per cent to 30 per cent in Turkey.

final say on Turkish policy in northern Iraq and on Cyprus. With the military clearly taking the back seat before the crucial 1 March vote, it was clear that the shaping of foreign policy was no longer made in the 'classic triangle' consisting of the prime minister, the foreign ministry and the military. Instead, the controversial decision was made exclusively by politicians. The Turkish Parliament, which was responsible for the decision, is traditionally *not* a key player in Turkish foreign policy. Another new trend was also noticeable; public opinion counted in Turkish foreign policy-making.

Another obvious change was the role of the President, whose opinion had earlier emerged as a fourth factor in the decision-making process on foreign policy in Turkey. This was no longer the case. President Ahmet Necdet Sezer (2000–2007) played a strictly limited role in foreign policy, unlike his predecessors Turgut Özal (1989–1993) and Süleyman Demirel (1993–2000). His reduced role was evident in the time running up to the invasion of Iraq in spring 2003. It was understandable, since his background was completely different. Both his predecessors had been prime minister before becoming presidents while Ahmet Necdet Sezer had a non-political, top-legal background. Once I had understood this change to the presidential role (which altered again with the election of Mr Gül), it became clear to me why the President chose to limit himself to the subject of Turkish–Swedish relations, leaving other foreign policy questions aside, during my first official visit to him.

Budding Turkish–Greek relations

Turkey's rapprochement with its Aegean rival, Greece, which took off in 1999, paved the way for Turkey's EU candidate status the same year. The Finnish EU Presidency worked very closely with the US government to achieve this outcome. It ultimately took a call from President Clinton aboard Air Force One to Prime Minister Ecevit in Ankara to get Turkey to take yes for an answer. The EU–Turkey breakthrough took place despite the unresolved issues of Cyprus and

Greco–Turkish disputes on territorial waters. Both were emotional political questions of national Turkish pride, often referred to as 'red lines'. The Greek government's support of the future Turkish EU membership was a reflection of the positive development achieved on these issues. The lobbying by the Greek conservative party (in power since March 2004), Nea Democratic, for the AK Party to become a member of the largest group in the European Parliament, the EPP,[1] was further evidence of the much improved relations between Turkey and Greece, all of which were spin-off effects of the EU 'pull factor'.

A new assertiveness

A new state of affairs had emerged in Turkey. The single majority government was enjoying strong popular support, growing prosperity and long sought-after EU membership talks, all of which were contributing to a new assertiveness in Turkish foreign policy. A pro-active and more independent-minded Middle Eastern policy was pursued, in particular towards Syria and the Hamas-led Palestinian government, which resulted in growing discontent in Washington. Among Turkish diplomats and politicians there was frustration and a sense of being continually misunderstood. They struggled to get across the message that it was important and necessary to maintain a dialogue with all Arab regimes, belonging as they did to Turkey's own, troubled region. 'One day the US will leave Iraq but we will still be here,' was a comment I often heard.[2] Prime Minister Erdoğan travelled extensively across the globe promoting the role of Turkey, both in political and commercial terms. Once the go-ahead to start EU negotiations was received in December 2004, he focused more on destinations beyond Europe. Sometimes a delegation with several

---

1.   The European People's Party (EPP) is made up of Christian Democrats and European Democrats, which constitute a total of 37 per cent of the European Parliament.

2.   See following chapter on 'Turkey's Role in the Middle East: Possibilities and Limitations'.

hundred Turkish businessmen accompanied him. Some businessmen did not hide the fact that it was the opportunity to talk with the prime minister, more than the final destination, which made the trip attractive to them. Erdoğan travelled to every continent, from Latin America to Africa, Australia and beyond. The pace, distances and number of destinations he covered were amazing.

The Bush administration's initial embrace of and positive attitudes towards the AK Party government cooled off as a result of the Iraq War. Turkey felt that neither were its security concerns properly addressed prior to the war, nor its warnings about the grave consequences of invading Iraq heeded. In a speech marking the two-year anniversary of the invasion, Secretary of Defense Rumsfeld openly blamed Turkey for the insurgency in Iraq turning out much stronger than anticipated, claiming that this was a result of Turkey blocking the US's Iraq strategy.[1] This view is widely shared within the US Government and is strongly held by Congress.

Since then, several mutual attempts have been made to close the gap between Ankara and Washington, in an effort to put an end to this turbulent period in US–Turkish relations. The challenge could perhaps be summarized in a favourite American saying of the experienced AK Party politician Mehmet Dülger, a Swiss-trained architect who was Head of the Foreign Policy Committee in Parliament between 2002–2007: 'Coming together is a beginning, staying together is progress, and working together is success.'[2]

Turkey as a hub

Turkey plays a direct role in a remarkable number of regions, of which many have mounting problems, especially the neighbouring Arab states. This is a fact often emphasized by Turkish diplomats well known and respected for their skills, as they deal with a fast-changing and

---

1.   TV interview on Fox News, Sunday 21 March 2005.
2.   Mehmet Dülger, 'Taking a Closer Look at Turkish–American Relations', in the *Turkish Policy Quarterly*, spring 2005.

more complex political environment than existed during the cold war. Western Europe, the Balkans, the Aegean and eastern Mediterranean, the Middle East, the Black Sea, the Caucasus and Central Asia are several of these sometimes overlapping regions. Occasionally, it was pointed out to me by Turkish diplomats and academics that coming from a country fortunate enough not to have had a war for almost two hundred years, I would not be able to quite comprehend the difficulties of living in a crisis-ridden hub like Turkey.

Russia and the Caucasus

The EU took centre stage in Turkish foreign politics during most of my time there, closely followed by increasing tensions with the US on a variety of important foreign policy issues. Russia, on the other hand, was seldom on top of the Turkish foreign policy agenda at the beginning of the new millennium. The energy project 'Blue Stream', a natural gas pipeline from Russia to Turkey, caused some troubles but its construction was completed in late 2002. Otherwise, growing commercial cooperation played an increasing part in relations between the two traditional arch-adversaries. In particular, the Turkish building industry was booming in Russia and in the oil-rich countries of the Caucasus.

The opening of a strategically important energy corridor between Azerbaijan and Turkey was a long-held US–Turkish vision, widely questioned on environmental and human rights grounds. Many believed it would remain an unfulfilled US–Turkish project. Refuting sceptics, the 1,770-kilometre pipeline was opened in May 2006, bringing Caspian oil from the Azeri capital Baku to the Turkish Mediterranean port of Ceyhan. The pipeline, circumventing Russia by crossing through Georgia, was viewed as a way to enhance stability in the region as well as reduce Western dependency on Middle Eastern oil.

It is possible that there might be a calculated effort to cultivate Russia as an alternative ally to the West, as part of a campaign for 'strategic depth'. There are, of course, limits to this idea because of serious differences on the issues of Cyprus, the PKK and Chechnya. But a Turkish 'Plan B', a coalition with Iran, Russia, India and China, as an alternative to Turkey's Western orientation, is troubling some top officials in the Pentagon.

US support for Turkey's EU bid

The US has given consistent support to Turkey's EU aspirations and efforts since the very beginning. The countries' shared values and common geopolitical interests underpinned US determined support for Turkish membership. The US position was clearly articulated to EU-country prime ministers before the Helsinki summit in 1999 and, even more so, before the 2002 Copenhagen summit, which pushed ajar a door to Turkish membership negotiations. Leading up to the historical EU decision in December 2004 to allow Turkey to initiate membership talks, the US was lobbying actively.

'Anything less than a full membership for Turkey would be a disappointment,' argued President Bush in a meeting in Washington with the Italian prime minister at the time, Berlusconi, on the day before the EU summit. 'Giving Turkey prospective membership would send an important message to the Islamic world,' was another American message vigorously conveyed by the US ambassador, Edelman, to EU colleagues in Ankara.

But the energetic US lobbying for Turkey caused some open murmurs of discontent. The French president at the time, Jacques Chirac, who at odds with his own party and the majority of the French population was actually supporting Turkey's EU bid, expressed his irritation during a NATO meeting in Istanbul in June 2004. He rebuked President Bush for urging the EU to give Turkey a firm date to start entry talks. The French president remarked that his US counterpart 'not only went too far but went into a domain which is not his own.' Similar feelings were noticeable elsewhere, including among EU colleagues in Ankara. The US took due account, fully aware of the risk of being counter-productive in its endorsement.

Eric Edelman, who became a top official in the Pentagon after leaving his ambassadorial post in Ankara in 2005, reiterated the US backing of Turkey's accession to the EU in a policy speech in Washington in summer 2006. 'The US will stand side-by-side with the Turkish people in support of their EU aspirations,'[1] he emphasized, while expressing confidence that Turkey would overcome the hurdles on its way towards the EU.

I heard about my former US colleague's remarks making headlines in the Turkish newspapers while I was visiting Batman. Sitting in a rustic café in the stifling heat under some of the few remaining old trees in the city centre, I recalled a phone call a few years earlier. One of the EU ambassadors in Ankara, a close friend of mine, rang to warn me about the escalating anti-American rhetoric, not so much among politicians as on the streets in Ankara. I was back home in Stockholm for a few days and my daughter was staying at the US residence with her best friend, Eric Edelman's daughter. My EU colleague rang to express concern about my daughter's security. I had no need to worry; she was in excellent hands. It illustrated, though, the intensity of feeling overshadowing US–Turkish relations from time to time, and the tough environment that US diplomats abroad could face.

The Ankara perspective

Turkey views EU membership and a genuine partnership with the US as fully complementary. One of Turkey's top diplomats, Ali Tuygan, argued eloquently that:

> A European Union that welcomes Turkey will ultimately demonstrate to itself and to the world at large that values such as democracy and rule of law are not specific to one religion

---

1.   Speech by Under Secretary of Defense for Policy, Ambassador Edelman, at the Washington Institute's Eighth Annual Turgut Özal Lecture, 19 June 2006.

or culture: that a civilization fault-line exists not among religions, but instead between democracy, modernity and reformism on the one side, and totalitarianism, radicalism and lethargy on the other. The United States has always been one of the steadiest supporters of Turkey's membership to the EU, exactly for the same reasons.[1]

Europe and the US will continue to need each other. Thus, a strong Europe in security matters and a robust NATO as an institutional embodiment of transatlantic links are viewed as mutually beneficial and therefore to be desired.

I found that there is genuine desire and willingness in Ankara to find ways to move forward and reinvigorate US–Turkish relations. It is necessary to seek an intensified dialogue between the two, in which Turkey is treated as an equal, and which will bring the countries increased understanding of each other's needs. This requires that developments in the past be firmly left behind, which will be a major challenge as long as there is uncertainty surrounding Iraq's trajectory.

Future US–Turkey–EU relations

'Turkey has learnt to speak up.' That was how a Turkish political journalist described to me his country's increasingly assertive foreign policy. Turkish foreign policy today is more aligned to the European mainstream than to the US position on a variety of key issues, such as Iraq, the Middle East Peace Process and global issues such as the Kyoto Protocol and the International Criminal Court (ICC). But the basis for US–Turkish relations should, after fifty years, be solid and comprehensive enough to withstand different policy positions.

Their mutual ambition to move forward and modernize relations was illustrated in the Strategic Vision Paper, outlined by Secretary of

---

1. Under-Secretary Ali Tuygan, 'The Present and Future of Turkish–American Relations: Ankara's Perspective', *Insight Turkey*, vol. 7, no. 1 Ankara Center for Turkish Policy Studies, 2005.

State Rice and Foreign Minister Gül in Ankara in spring 2006, and finalized a few months later. It created a framework for cooperation on global terrorism, democratization, combating organized crime and other issues through a mechanism of consultations.

Former US Ambassador to Turkey Mark Parris said in 2005 that 'Washington will always find it easier to work with Turkey than around Turkey.'[1] This might well prove to be the case. The growing schism between the West and the Muslim world is confronting foreign policy-makers not only in Washington and Brussels but also across continents.

A renewed and deepened appreciation of the strategic importance of US–Turkish relations could, over time, be brought about by Turkey's role in helping to foster a better understanding between European, transatlantic and Muslim societies.

---

1.   Mark Parris, 'Allergic Partners: Can US–Turkish Relations be Saved?', *Turkish Policy Quarterly*, vol. 4, no. 1, spring 2005.

NINE

Turkey's Role in the Middle East: Possibilities and Limitations

Mutual scepticism

As I was finishing my posting as ambassador in Lebanon and preparing for my transfer to Turkey, I embarked on the traditional circle of farewell visits to the top political leaders and other key persons in society. One of them, a Muslim educated at a Christian school in Beirut, had opened my eyes to the many similarities between Islam and Christianity. His reaction to my move to Ankara was not one of conspicuous tolerance. Immediately he recalled how his grandmother, a Shiʻi Muslim, had been discriminated against by the Ottomans, as a result of which he would never visit Turkey unless it was absolutely necessary. Events that took place almost one hundred years ago clearly still played a prominent role in his mind.

The close historical, geographical and cultural ties between Turkey and the Arab Middle East loosened after the end of World War I and the dissolution of the Ottoman Empire. New nation states were created by Western powers out of what had been sprawling provinces of the Ottoman Empire. Separation between Turkey and the Middle East followed in various areas.

The abolition of the Arabic alphabet in Turkey (in 1928) manifested a cultural as well as a religious separation, as Arabic is the language of the Qur'an. Another act of dissociation from the Arabs was the abolition of the Caliphate, which had been founded on the idea of a united political leadership across the Muslim world. But the Islamic world became politically divided early on. Political disintegration had occurred already after the fall of the Umayyad, the first Arabic-Islamic dynasty,[1] and it culminated after the fall of Baghdad in 1258, when the Mongol Empire captured the city. Throughout the centuries the Caliphate remained a politically unfulfilled vision until it was abolished in the early twentieth century. Atatürk's removal of the Constantinople-based[2] Caliphate[3] was part of the secularization of the new republican Turkey and eliminated a 1,350-year-old Islamic institution. It shook Muslims from Morocco in the west to Indonesia in the east. 'It's the equivalent to the Vatican in Rome suddenly being closed down,' said one Muslim friend in Istanbul, trying to explain to me the impact it had had.

The Caliphate has resurfaced in current political debates. US Vice President Cheney, Defense Secretary Rumsfeld and other top officials in Washington have warned that al-Qa'ida's ultimate goal is to re-establish the Caliphate throughout the entire Muslim world, to be 'governed by sharia law, the most rigid interpretation of the Koran.'[4]

---

1. Umayyad period, AD 661–750.
2. Constantinople officially became Istanbul in 1930.
3. Following the death of the Prophet Muhammad, caliphs (*calipha* is Arabic for 'successor') were appointed to the leadership. When the Ottomans conquered Egypt in 1517 Sultan Selim I assumed the title and became Caliph without the Ottomans taking on the overall political leadership. The Ottomans' Sultans retained the title until the Caliphate was abolished in 1924 by Kemal Atatürk.
4. Quote from Vice President Cheney's speech in Lake Elmo, Minnesota, September 2004. 'Watchword of the Day: Beware the Caliphate', in the *International Herald Tribune*, 12 December 2005.

That argument has been widely dismissed by academics,[1] who claim it is a threat beyond anything Osama Bin Laden can deliver.

Turkey's integration following World War II into the West, with membership of NATO and key European institutions, emphasized its move away from its Ottoman and Islamic past. The unique relationship between Turkey and the Jewish state of Israel further highlighted the anomaly of Turkey's situation in the region. Turkey was among the first countries to recognize the state of Israel,[2] but its close-knit and unique strategic relations with Israel were forged much later, in the mid-1990s. The special Turkish–Jewish relationship goes back more than five hundred years. It dates from the time when the Ottomans opened their doors for Jews who had been forced to leave Spain in 1492 on orders from the Spanish King Ferdinand and Queen Isabella.

The deep Arab disregard towards the Turks, stemming in particular from the latter parts of the Ottoman era, was not one-sided, but rather mutual. In Turkey, a widespread habit prevailed of viewing the Arab Middle East as backward, lacking in democracy and struggling with religious fundamentalism.

Professor Elisabeth Özdalga from the prestigious METU University in Ankara has highlighted the need in Turkey to improve knowledge of the Arabic language as well as of Arabic literature, history and society. Academic neglect and ignorance of Arab culture and society have contributed to a prevalent disrespect for Arabs, noticeable among strictly secular nationalists and nationalists supporting Turkish Islam, according to Professor Özdalga's research.[3]

Changing perceptions

However, guarded relations on both sides are starting to change in the wake of increasingly frequent political crises in the region and a

1. See article mentioned above.
2. On 28 March 1949.
3. Elisabeth Özdalga, 'The Hidden Arab: A Critical Reading of the Notion of 'Turkish Islam', *Middle Eastern Studies*, vol. 42, no. 4, July 2006, pp. 551–570.

new, proactive and assertive stance on Middle Eastern policy by the AK Party government. The Party's Islamic roots have had a reassuring effect on Muslim Arabs, who believed that the secularization of the Turkish republic had resulted in a loss of its Muslim identity.

The democratization of Turkey is closely followed by all in the Middle East. Turkish top diplomats like to point out that there were more journalists from the Middle East than from Europe at the EU summit in Brussels in 2004, when Turkey, as the first Muslim-populated country, was given permission to start membership talks. The fascination felt throughout the Middle East for Turkey's endeavours to join the European Union is intense.

The change of government in Turkey in 2002 shifted the balance to a degree in Turkish–Israeli–Palestinian relations, but without threatening the close Turkish–Israeli ties.

Turkey's Middle Eastern policy has become increasingly ambitious and high profile. It is likely to be further enhanced with Mr Gül as president, as he speaks Arabic after many years of working in Saudi Arabia and he has a remarkable network and standing in the region after his time as foreign minister. But with a deteriorating situation in the conflict-ridden region and the Iraq War adding complexity to the Kurdish issue in Turkey, it is far from clear if that will be an asset or burden in Turkey's quest to join the EU.

Turkey's unique relations with Israel

The then Israeli prime minister, Ariel Sharon, faced by a second Palestinian intifada and increasing isolation in the Middle East, visited Ankara in summer 2001. He arrived in the only country in the region where he would be warmly welcomed. Relations between Turkey and Israel, both democratic pro-Western and non-Arab countries, had deepened in the 1990s when a unique alliance was forged between the two countries. Their close ties with the US created a new, triangular strategic alliance in the post-cold war era between Washington, Ankara and Jerusalem. High-level political and diplomatic visits, intelligence sharing and joint military exercises followed. Israeli president Ezer Weizman, for example, visited Turkey for his third time as president in only five years, in autumn 1999.[1]

Turkey's strategic relations with Israel are more far-reaching than those most EU countries have. It was described as a strategic alliance, that is, the same as Turkey's relations with the US, on the website of the Turkish Foreign Ministry in the late 1990s. Five-year agreements on military cooperation, first signed in 1996, included plans such as inter alia joint training and separate exercises in each other's territory. However, close military cooperation with Israel has not been uncontroversial.

Initially, there was trepidation in Israel about the newly elected, Turkish Islamic-rooted government. However, Israel and the powerful Jewish lobby in Washington were given reassurances about the AK Party's democratic credentials by influential Jewish Turks. Ishak Alaton, one of Turkey's leading businessmen, was one of them. The self-made industrialist was a vocal and long-standing EU supporter and friend of Israel. In his youth he spent a few years in Sweden, working as a welder. Fifty years later, he was still keenly interested and knowledgeable about Sweden and able to speak Swedish fluently. Sometimes Ishak Alaton is referred to as 'Sweden's permanent ambassador in Turkey'. His business empire is based in a former royal residence on a hilltop in Istanbul, overlooking the Bosporus. There, numerous foreign delegations have met over the years with Mr Alaton, who always enthusiastically explains and lobbies for Turkey.

Reassurances on Turkey's direction under its new government were followed up by Mr Erdoğan's visit to the US in early 2003, which

---

1.   The first visit, in January 1994, was the first ever by an Israeli head of state and included his signing agreements on culture, education, science and sports. *Timeline of Turkish–Israeli Relations, 1949–2006* (Washington Institute for Near Eastern Policy).

included crucial meetings in New York with key Jewish organizations. After terror attacks in Istanbul in November that year, targeting synagogues, the British Consulate and a British bank, Prime Minister Erdoğan visited the chief rabbi of the Turkish Jewish community, marking the first such visit in Turkish history.

Israeli support for Turkey's EU bid

Israel always supported Turkey's EU integration, believing it would safeguard Turkey as a Western ally and prevent Islamic fundamentalism from spreading. Israel's acting Prime Minister Shimon Peres sent letters to several EU leaders and parliamentarians in November 1995, expressing support for Turkey's Customs Union with the EU. This strong support was not long-lasting, but with the escalating Israeli–Palestinian conflict, Israel's role became more controversial. It kept a substantially lower profile leading up to the historic EU summit in 2004, when it was decision-time for Turkey's membership talks.

Israel–Palestine conflict

A number of incidents had, however, occurred to dampen Turkish–Israeli relations. The Israeli assassination of Hamas's founder, Sheikh Yassin, in March 2004 enraged Prime Minister Erdoğan. He denounced the killing of the crippled spiritual leader, which took place outside a mosque after Friday prayers, as a 'terrorist act'. US and Israeli reactions were 'incredibly strong', recalled a close party colleague of the prime minister who was travelling with him in Japan at the time. A few months later, Prime Minister Erdoğan criticized Israel's policy in Gaza, describing it as 'state-sponsored terrorism.'

Following Hamas's sweeping and surprising victory in the Palestinian election in January 2006, the Turkish prime minister maintained that the international community must respect the

Palestinians' decision. 'Democracy is a regime of tolerance,'[1] he stressed, while making a strong appeal to Hamas to renounce terror and drop its policy of non-recognition of Israel. 'It is time for Hamas to move from the margins to the centre,' he said.

The EU took a different position, distancing itself from Hamas, which was designated a terror organization by Europe in 2003. Hamas had to renounce violence and recognize Israel in order to maintain ties with Europe, stated top EU officials. Meanwhile, the Turkish foreign minister, Gül, urged Hamas to 'act in a democratic way.' A visiting Hamas delegation, hosted by Turkish officials in Ankara in February 2006, resulted in strong resentment in Israel and in the US. It added to growing doubts over Turkey's relations with Israel.

Having worked on the Middle East peace process for many years in the 1990s, my impression from numerous meetings with Prime Minister Erdoğan and Foreign Minister Gül was that they seemed to differ from many other leaders in the region. They appeared genuinely committed to finding a solution to the Israel–Palestine conflict in speaking out beyond the call of political correctness about the necessity of solving the Palestinian question. Tayyip Erdoğan and Abdullah Gül had both put their political prestige on the line by reiterating Turkey's willingness to act as a mediator to facilitate the stalled Middle East peace process. These offers to complement already existing mechanisms were often met with silence. However, the Turkish aspiration to play an active role in trying to end one of the world's longest-running conflicts was not new. It was a long-held ambition in Turkish diplomatic circles, which enjoyed a broad and well-deserved respect.

Turkey was viewed as a fair player by both parties in the conflict. It was not a coincidence that Mahmoud Abbas, shortly after his election as Palestinian president, went to Ankara in early 2005 on his first trip abroad. The Palestinian leader met his Israeli counterpart, President

---

1. 'PM Erdoğan Says Hamas Should be Given a Chance', *Turkish Daily News*, 28 January 2006.

Peres, for the first time in six years in a meeting that took place in Ankara in November 2007. Together they addressed the Turkish Parliament. It was a unique event with an Israeli president speaking for the first time in a Parliament in a Muslim country. President Peres was signalling the Israeli wish to have Turkey as a player in the Israeli–Palestinian peace process.

The majority of Turks are Sunni Muslims, like the Palestinians. It would, though, be too simplistic to view Turkish endeavours to effect a peace agreement between Israel and an independent Palestine as purely a sign of Sunni solidarity. It is as much a reflection of Turkey's long-standing and successful strategy of maintaining excellent relations with Israel and Palestine, unique in the region.

Previous critical positions for Turkey

Incidents denting the traditionally solid relationship between Turkey and Israel were sometimes portrayed as new occurrences and as by-products of Turkey's pro-Islamic government. For these reasons, criticism of Israel by Turkish governments was often overlooked. The AK Party government's immediate predecessor, a staunchly secular government up until 2002, was at times even harsher in its objections to Israeli policy towards the Palestinians. In a joint press conference in Ankara in 2001, the left-wing Turkish premier, Ecevit, rejected Prime Minister Sharon's claim that the Palestinian leader Arafat 'supports terror'. Less than a year later, in spring 2002, Mr Ecevit described Sharon's policy towards the Palestinians as 'genocide', resulting in a chorus of criticism in Israel.

Flourishing economic ties

If Turkish–Israeli political relations are strained at times, they do not seem to lose ground in the economic domain, facilitated by a free trade agreement which has been in effect since 1997. A significant agreement was reached in spring 2004, committing Israel to importing huge amounts of water from Turkey's Manavgat River during a twenty-year period. The Turkish purchase of Israeli high-tech military equipment means that defence deals form a large share of bilateral trade. Turkey was Israel's largest trade partner in the region during 2005, importing 900 million dollars in goods from Israel and exporting 1.2 billion dollars in goods.

In addition, Turkey is an increasingly popular tourist destination for Israelis, who have limited choices of places to visit in the region. During my first visit to Antalya on the Mediterranean coast on a winter's day, I learnt that retired Israelis represent the majority of the tourist trade when the summer season is over and the northern Europeans have left. To my surprise, the area could offer swimming in the sea as well as downhill skiing during the winter. Until then, I had thought only Lebanon could offer that combination around the Mediterranean.

Quagmire in Iraq

It was early February 2003 and hope was rapidly fading that an invasion of Iraq could be avoided. The soon-to-be-prime minister Tayyip Erdoğan was deeply concerned. He supported bringing an end to Saddam Hussein's regime but strongly warned against a war in Iraq, which turned out to be only six weeks away. 'There will be fighting on the streets of Baghdad, from house to house, and sectarian violence,' he predicted during a meeting with the Swedish foreign minister, Anna Lindh, in the AK Party headquarters. The subject of the meeting was serious but the atmosphere was exceptionally good. The short, blonde and vivacious Social Democrat Anna Lindh, widely known for her support for human rights in Turkey, greeted the serene, towering conservative Turkish prime minister-to-be saying 'If I was Turkish I would have voted for you.' It was the only time I ever saw Mr Erdoğan taken aback, but only for a fleeting moment.

The Turkish government was under immense pressure to make a decision on transiting US troops through its territory, enabling an entry into Iraq along the 220-kilometre mountainous border with Turkey. The Turkish military, unusually, were taking the back seat, emphasizing that it was a decision for the politicians to make. One top general said to me that whatever decision would be made, 'it will only be the US's war, never Turkey's', even if Turkey in the end decided to allow US attacks from the Turkish–Iraqi border. 'The Turkish military will concentrate on humanitarian work for the refugees during the war,' he predicted, a month before the war broke out. 'Unlike the first Gulf War in 1991, the refugees will remain in northern Iraq and not enter into Turkey,' he said. There turned out to be no flow of refugees, contrary to the assessments made by international humanitarian organizations and many governments.

The Turkish rejection of transiting US troops deeply scarred its relations with the US. The divide within the EU on Iraq was more public and went deeper than any other previous foreign policy issue. Several years after the outbreak of the war, Iraq remains a nightmare for Turkey. In a worst-case scenario, the instability there has the potential to become a full-scale civil war and to dismember Iraq, which could terminally damage Turkey's EU process.

The Kurds as a regional issue

Turkey is unanimous in its policy on Iraq; its territorial integrity must remain unchanged. 'A federated structure in Iraq based on ethnicity or religious sects will not be healthy. It will bother Syria, Iran and Turkey,'[1] warned Prime Minister Erdoğan during a visit to the US in 2004.[2] The same message was given repeatedly to the EU countries. It is a 'red line' for the Turkish government and establishment alike.

The Kurds are the world's largest ethnic group without an independent state. With growing instability and uncertainty about

---

1. These three countries have an estimated 7–20 per cent Kurds among their populations. In Iraq, where the total figure is 15–20 per cent, a Kurdistani region was established in 2006 within the federal state.
2. Speech at the Council of Foreign Relations in New York, 26 January 2004.

Iraq's political future, there is fear in Turkey of the dismemberment of Iraq, resulting in an independent Kurdistan in the north and with potential long-term consequences for Kurdish-dominated southeastern Turkey. Despite US reassurances that it will not happen, there is a lingering deep concern among Turks of a future 'new Israel' being created for Kurds, who turned out to be the US's most reliable Iraqi allies.

When the EU pushes for cultural rights for the Kurds, as part of their human rights reforms, it is surprisingly often mistaken for support of the establishment of an independent Kurdish state. There is no such support by any EU country government. During my early days in Ankara, the most common question I received at public meetings was why Sweden supported the PKK. 'We never did and never will,' was always my answer. After a unanimous EU – Sweden included – labelled the PKK a terror organization, the issue rarely resurfaced. It was amazing how quickly the information on that decision made in Brussels spread and was appreciated by ordinary Turks. Subsequently, the most frequent question put to me was an inquiry as to when IKEA, the Swedish-owned furniture company, would open a store in Turkey. (They actually did in 2005.)

Renewed violence by Kurdish separatists in Turkey highlighted the problem of the PKK bases in northern Iraq, estimated to harbour up to 5,000 militants. US opposition to Turkish military raids against the PKK in northern Iraq is incomprehensible to most Turks. They find it inconsistent with the US-led 'war on terror' in Iraq and elsewhere. The Bush administration's support of the sustained, thirty-four-day Israeli bombardments of Lebanon, aiming to defeat Hezbollah, added to the confusion and resentment of the US position vis-à-vis the PKK in Iraq. 'Why is Turkey not allowed to deal with the PKK in Iraq if Israel can deal with Hezbollah in Lebanon?,' a well-known and moderate Turkish journalist asked me rhetorically in the summer of 2006. There are few regrets in Turkey for not having participated in the invasion of Iraq, although it led to a frustrating lack of leverage on the US and the situation in northern Iraq. Despite there having been no Turkish participation in the Iraq War, there have been one hundred Turkish fatalities, among them many truck drivers, since the outbreak of the war.[1]

A top Turkish politician told me shortly after the end of the inconclusive Israel–Lebanon war that it showed that a terror organization or guerrilla movement cannot be entirely defeated. The Turkish military will never invade northern Iraq on a large scale to combat the PKK, he emphasized. A completely successful mission is unlikely, as the Israeli example illustrated. The price for Turkey would also be too high as regards the EU and the US, he said reassuringly. He ruled out the possibility that the Turkish military would invade northern Iraq without the prior consent of the Turkish government.

Iran

Turkey and Iran, both with large Kurdish populations, share anxiety about the future of Iraq. Both vehemently oppose the idea of an independent Kurdish state in northern Iraq. Other aspects shaping their relations are their distinctly contrasting governments; a democratic and secular government in Ankara and a theocratic, Islamic government in Tehran. Their respective relations with Israel and the US are further examples of radically different policies between Turkey and Iran. Their conflicting interests in Central Asia and the Caucasus are also aspects influencing Turkish–Iranian relations. At the same time, Turkey has a vital and developing economic trade with Iran. A natural gas deal in summer 2006 to export gas in pipelines to Europe via Turkish territory is one example of a significant commercial agreement.

Turkey has adopted an active regional approach, aiming to minimize the problems with its neighbouring countries, including

---

1.   Written reply in Parliament by Turkish Foreign Minister Gül in July 2006.

Iran, while trying to avoid confrontations in the international arena. The EU's twin-track strategy on Iran's nuclear programme, seeking to maintain a dialogue with Tehran while not excluding future UN sanctions, is similar to Turkey's pragmatic approach. The Iranian enrichment of uranium is not considered an existential threat by Turkey, which constitutes yet another fault line between Turkey and the US in a key foreign policy area. Washington, like Israel, views Iran as an existential threat to the region and beyond.

In 2002, some top Turkish military officials grabbed the headlines by suggesting that Turkey should abandon its efforts to join the EU and instead turn towards Iran and Russia. In diplomatic circles in Ankara it was generally interpreted as a test to gauge the reactions of the EU and the US, possibly to shake up Turkey's frustratingly slow EU membership process. The proposal was put forward by a small group of generals, among them the Secretary General, Tuncer Kılınç of the powerful Turkish National Security Council, shortly before the EU summit in Copenhagen in December 2002. Turkey had attached high hopes of getting a starting date at that summit for membership talks to begin, which did not materialize.

It was an astonishing initiative, especially considering that the Turkish military is traditionally the safeguard of Atatürk's revered policy of staunch secularism and a European vision for Turkey. Turning to the Islamic, theocratic regime in Iran as an option was undoubtedly an unexpected alternative coming from top military men.

The idea of a Turkish–Iranian–Russian alliance resurfaced in the Turkish debate as Turkey's EU process slowed down after accession talks started in 2005 and scepticism towards Turkish membership grew among EU countries such as France and Germany.

Lebanon: A new atmosphere

Relations between Turkey and Lebanon underwent a slow process of improvement for some years, which 'all happened to fall into place' during the AK Party's time in government. 'We wanted a new atmosphere,' recalled a top Turkish diplomat during a briefing for the EU member states in 2004.

After the inconclusive Israel–Lebanon war in August 2006, UN peacekeepers disembarked on the shores of southern Lebanon with Europeans among the first to touch the shore and making up the majority of the reinforcements for the international mission. While Turkey was initially expected to take a leading role, an unexpected turn of events unfolded at home. The sending of peacekeeping forces to Lebanon turned into a domestic controversy, with President Sezer voicing his strong opposition to a Turkish deployment, supported by the main opposition party, the CHP. There were claims that sending troops to Lebanon would undermine efforts to combat PKK violence in Turkey. Thousands of demonstrators in the streets also argued that Turkey would be put in the position of protecting Israel's interests while endangering Muslim lives.

Meanwhile, Israeli Prime Minister Olmert as well as leading Lebanese figures spoke out in favour of Turkish troops, illustrating Turkey's unique role in the region. The Lebanese EU professor Chibli Mallat, argued for a robust Turkish contingent in the Turkish press.[1] Turkey had largely turned its back on the Middle East during the twentieth century, while the Middle East continued to solicit Turkey's return, whether to deal with the Kurdish problem, Iraq or the impact of Islamism on Turkish politics, he noted. Turkish participation in helping Lebanon into a new, lasting peace would draw a historical line for Turkey of unprecedented magnitude, and position it squarely as a Middle Eastern power. Professor Mallat also believed it would accelerate the Turkish EU membership process, with Turkey working alongside France in the UN forces.

On the eve of the decision, I had dinner with a leading AK Party foreign policy law-maker. 'We simply have to participate if we want to play a role in the region,' was his conclusion. He viewed the criticism as mere attempts to score political goals on the domestic arena, a view

---

1.   Daily newspaper *Sabah*, 4 August 2006.

reiterated by the then Minister of Justice Cemil Çiçek shortly before the crucial vote in Parliament. It was a confident AK Party leadership which brought the motion on peacekeeping troops to Parliament. There were few doubts of a repeat of the surprising rejection by Parliament of US troop deployment in Turkey shortly before the Iraqi invasion. The vote was passed with a large majority.

Turkey's enhanced involvement in the Middle East was yet again illustrated during the political crises in Lebanon in November 2007 when the deeply divided Lebanese leadership struggled to agree on a new president. Prime Minister Erdoğan was in daily telephone contact with Beirut, trying to assist the beleaguered country.

A new chapter with Syria

Turkey's ties with Syria went from bordering on war in the late 1990s (over Syria's protection of the then at-large PKK leader Öcalan) to close and frequent top-level contact between Ankara and Damascus. Hard and discreet work by Turkish diplomats and politicians had obtained results. Syria is viewed by Turkey as one of the least problematic countries in the Middle East. When Syria was implicated in the murder of former Lebanese Premier Rafik Hariri, Turkey actively encouraged the Syrian regime to fully cooperate with the UN investigation into the 2004 assassination.

President Bashar al-Assad and his wife's state visit to Turkey in early 2004 was soon reciprocated by President Sezer's visit to Damascus, further increasing the irritation between Turkey and the US. Turkey's fostering of its relations with Syria continued, despite strong opposition from the Bush administration. The first lady of Syria, the young English-born Asma al-Assad, quickly became a favourite of the glossy women's magazines in Turkey.

Turkey's Middle Eastern policy: Asset or burden in the EU process?

While pressing for EU accession, Turkey has deepened its ties with the Arab world. Its relations with Israel remain close despite recurrent tensions, in particular on questions relating to Hamas. The Turkish proactive neighbourhood policy was reflected in the AK government's ambition to improve ties with the Arab League. Turkey became the first country to request and be granted a status as 'permanent guest' at the twenty-two-member-state Arab League, based in the region's most populous state, Egypt.

Increasing instability in the region and the unresolved Israel–Palestine conflict are straining Turkey's regional interests and choices. They also create potential pitfalls for Turkey's EU accession with northern Iraq and the Kurdish question being the most obvious stumbling-block. Turkey has so far skilfully navigated its policy of dialogue and cooperation in the Middle East while remaining in harmony with the EU's foreign policy. At times its success has been as a result of the lack of common EU foreign policy, with the Iraq War being a noticeable example.

Meanwhile, Turkey's standing in the region has been enhanced due to its efforts to reform and to join the EU. Its ability to absorb a mildly Islamist government which champions reform in order to join the EU was praised by the well-known Arab columnist Rami Khouri, who described the democratic and secular Turkey as 'a beacon of light in the Middle East'.[1]

The EU is by far the largest donor to the Palestinian people. It is sometimes, though, described as a paymaster without political clout in the Middle East, unlike the US. Muslim-populated Turkey is pursuing EU membership while deepening its ties with the Middle East. It is addressing core issues such as democratization and human rights, often overlooked in the Arab Middle East. Turkey has the potential not only to become a local 'honest broker', adding to the impact and influence of the EU, but also an admired example in the region.

---

1. Rami G. Khouri, 'The Lessons of a Predominantly Middle Eastern Turkey', in the Lebanese newspaper *The Daily Star*, 3 May 2006.

TEN

Turkey: Bridge or Barrier
Between East and West?

Following the two world wars, reconciliation between Germany and France became the biggest challenge in Europe in the twentieth century. To build a bridge between the West and Islam might well turn out to be the biggest challenge during this century. Turkey, as a thriving secular democracy, with an overwhelmingly Muslim population among its 72 million inhabitants, could hold the key to increased understanding and tolerance between East and West. It is unique in being the only EU candidate country with a mainly Muslim population. Chris Patten, the EU Commissioner for External Affairs from 1999 until November 2004, took an early lead in arguing for Turkey's importance as a bridge between the West and the Islamic world and suggesting that the EU should reach out to Turkey.

The terror attacks against the US on 11 September 2001 sent shock waves through the world. The Turkish state was taken less by surprise than most countries, having fought its own difficult war on terrorism against the militant PKK organization for more than fifteen years. There was great sympathy within Turkey for the US, mixed with a sense of belated justification for its own war on terrorism, which had led to extensive criticism over the years from the international community on human rights grounds. The Turkish political and military leadership believed to a great extent that its terrorist war had been fought without any understanding, only severe criticism from the West, which until the 9/11 attacks lacked first-hand experience of large and ongoing loss of lives in terrorist acts, the UK being the only exception.

Shortly after the terror attacks in the US, I paid a courtesy call to the military headquarters in central Ankara as part of the familiarization tour of an ambassador to a new posting. I was received by the second-highest ranking general in Turkey, Yaşar Büyükanit, who was later promoted, as expected, to take the helm of the General Staff in August 2006. He briefed me vigorously for a full hour about the terror threats facing Turkey. In a friendly but matter-of-fact atmosphere, he presented a brand-new, thick document, with a plane heading straight into the World Trade Center in New York on its front page, containing lists of suspected terrorist organizations in different countries. Among them were several, presumably Kurdish, based in Sweden, although one, consisting of a housewives' association in an immigrant-dense suburb of Stockholm, came across as far-fetched to me. Much later I learned that there had been cases of immigrants being coerced into giving financial contributions to the PKK, otherwise their relatives living in Turkey would suffer, they were told. But the military's document on terrorism that he handed over to me reflected the starkly different realities with which a Turk and a Western European live. The gap between us suddenly felt very wide as I sat in the ornate and gilded military headquarters, where the top general was elaborating on terrorism and the EU. He fully supported Turkish membership but envisioned a remarkably long wait. In the end, this might turn out to be the most accurate prediction.

Post 9/11, focus fell on Turkey's role as a potential bridge-builder between East and West in the wake of the US-led 'war against terror' while at the same time fostering democracy in the Middle East. This became a cornerstone of US foreign policy. When the first formal review of US foreign policy since the invasion of Iraq was presented in March 2006, President Bush described the struggle against militant Islamism as the 'great ideological conflict of the early years of the twenty-first century.' Can Turkey, with its EU accession process, become living proof to refute Samuel Huntington's claim of 'clashes of civilizations'? Despite its controversy, his phrase has obviously struck a chord, as illustrated by the frequency with which it is quoted and used in argument.

Clash of civilizations

The American Professor Huntington was in the audience when Prime Minister Erdoğan disputed his controversial argument on 'clashes between civilizations', in which democracy depends on the cultural fault line dividing the West and the Muslim world. The Turkish prime minister gave a speech at Harvard, the professor's own Ivy League university, firmly rejecting his assertion that democracy is incompatible with Middle Eastern culture and religion. Turkey, a secular democracy whose population is largely Muslim, is evidence that that is not true, the prime minister stated in his speech, which was delivered in Turkish to a packed auditorium. He stressed that there is an unmistakable demand in the Middle East and in the wider Muslim world for democratization, although not necessarily with the Western cultural trappings associated with it. At the same time, the Turkish prime minister warned against the practice of democracy being watered down under the guise of respect for regional differences. Like Western democracy, Middle Eastern democracies must not merely be limited to elections and parliaments, but be built around respect for human rights and freedoms, rule of law, gender equality and transparency in governments. 'The purpose cannot be to create self-styled democracies, but rather encourage steps that are conducive to establishing democratic rule at universal standards.'

One of Mr Erdoğan's close advisers, who accompanied him on

the multi-stop visit to the US in January 2004, recalled the Harvard keynote speech to me upon returning to Ankara, without hiding his satisfaction that Huntington had been present to listen to the Turkish case. During the question–answer session, Professor Huntington never took the floor. In introducing the Turkish prime minister, Turkey was described as a critically important ally and an example. 'Turkey bridges worlds desperately in need of understanding'.[1] Mr Erdoğan called for an 'Istanbul Process' that would link Europe, the US and the Middle East together in an effort to boost democratic government, promote economic growth and ensure security in the troubled region. Istanbul is the only city in the world straddling two continents, where a boat trip on the Bosporus shows Asia just off the starboard and Europe off the port bow.

The Istanbul Process stumbled later the same year, when a Turkish initiative to hold a conference in Istanbul between the EU countries and the fifty-seven-member-state organization of Muslim countries, the Organization of the Islamic Conference (OIC), was abruptly cancelled in 2004. The EU Presidency at the time, the Netherlands, took a brisk lead in calling off the meeting several days before it was planned to start. Traditionally, attempts to find compromises are kept up until the very end, which was not the case this time, surprising and disappointing several of the other EU states. The controversy was about the status of the Turkish Cypriots. They were prevented from participating as observers at the EU–OIC conference because of a sign on the conference table reading 'Turkish Federal State of Cyprus', despite the fact that this formulation was used in the United Nations Kofi Annan Plan for Cyprus.

On the same day that the conference was supposed to start, the Swedish foreign minister and I went to see the incoming OIC Secretary General, the Turkish Professor Ekmeleddin Ishanoğlu, at the academic institute he was in charge of, housed in a small, exquisite

---

1. Professor Graham Allison in his introduction of the guest speaker, PM Erdoğan on 30 January 2004. *Harvard University Gazette*, 5 February 2004.

Ottoman palace in the centre of Istanbul. He showed remarkable self-restraint in holding back his disappointment at the EU. The frustration was more visible within the Foreign Ministry in Ankara, where thorough and time-consuming preparations had been carried out in vain. Building bridges assumes that there is a mutual willingness to have a dialogue. That time, the EU failed the test.

If the EU–OIC conference was cancelled due to political difficulties over Cyprus, the two organizations had scored better at a similar forum a few years earlier, only months after the 9/11 terror attacks. The EU–OIC Joint Forum, held in Turkey in February 2002, brought together 76 countries and 51 foreign ministers, who met to discuss how to intensify a multicultural and inter-religious dialogue. It was the first major encounter in the aftermath of the 11 September terrorist attacks, and was the brainchild of the visionary Foreign Minister Ismail Cem. He seemed more comfortable during intellectual challenges, such as the discussions at the Forum, than in the tough political environment of the Turkish coalition government that he was part of at the time. Istanbul, on the shores of the Bosporus, where people commute daily between Europe and Asia, signifies the unique position of the city, noted Prime Minister Ecevit as the preparations for the conference were underway. The EU's High Representative for foreign policy, Dr Javier Solana, highlighted the importance of identifying the gaps in our respective perceptions of each other. He mentioned the status of women as one example, warning against clichés, while praising Turkey and Tunisia for their long-term reforms. Capital punishment, which the EU is continually trying to push for an end to, was also mentioned. At the time, Turkey still had the death penalty and it was generally regarded as politically impossible to abolish this as long as the PKK leader Öcalan was imprisoned and not yet executed.

It was a conference full of hope and expectations. Dr Solana expressed the EU's commitment towards recreating Afghanistan as 'a country of peace'. He sent greetings to the absent vice president of the

OIC, Yasser Arafat, who was unable to leave his crumbling Ramallah headquarters, and was calling for a 'two-state solution' for Israelis and Palestinians, something that the EU had restated its determination to work towards. Iraq, then still under Saddam Hussein's regime, was represented by its newly appointed foreign minister, Naji Sabri, whom I was trying to locate among all the hundreds of participants to discuss a bilateral issue. But he was difficult to find since his face was unfamiliar to most participants at the conference, myself included.

The 9/11 terror attacks highlighted the stark notion that some clearly wanted the new millennium to begin as a clash of civilizations. By participating in the conference in Istanbul, many of the top level participants wanted to show their desire not to allow this prophecy to become reality. The renowned English professor, Bernard Lewis, recalled how the long-standing relationship between Christendom and Islam was mostly one of conflicts, but outlined that the core of the problem was their similarities rather than their differences. The two religions' common ancestry, common background and to a large degree common beliefs had created rivalry, especially with both making claims to the same geographical area. Professor Lewis, a man in his eighties whose frailty was overshadowed by his strong convictions, pointed out that the West and the Middle East traditionally agreed in their definition of bad government as oppression and tyranny, while their definitions of good government usually differed. In the West, it was usually defined as freedom, while in the Islamic world it was about justice. Professor Lewis appealed for the two to join forces against a common enemy of ignorance, bigotry, poverty, tyranny, terror and underdevelopment.

The Organization of the Islamic Conference (OIC) showed the political solidarity of the Muslim world towards the Turkish Cypriots when its leader at the time, Abdelvahid Belkeziz, became the first top official from an international organization to visit the Turkish Republic of Northern Cyprus in spring 2004. He brought 'a salute and love from the world's 1.5 billion Muslims' to the internationally isolated Turkish Cypriots, who faced continued isolation when the UN plan for reunification of the island failed after the Greek Cypriot rejection in the 24 April 2004 referendum. The island's future remains a major divider and stumbling block to EU–Turkish relations, which was yet again highlighted at the EU summit in December 2006 when Turkey's membership talks were partially suspended after Ankara's refusal to open its ports to Cyprus.

The OIC is the only body that has the capacity to speak on behalf of the Muslim world. It is significant that for the first time since the OIC was established in 1969, Turkey succeeded in having one of its citizens appointed as secretary-general of the organization in 2004 after a skilful campaign, spearheaded by the Turkish foreign ministry. Turkey had tried some years previously with the very able ambassador Yaşar Yakiş as a candidate (who later became foreign minister), but failed. Turkey was regarded as too secular a state at the time and therefore 'lost', several Middle Eastern diplomats explained to me.

Two years after the AK Party came to power, the Turkish professor, Ihsanoğlu, like Ambassador Yakiş a fluent Arabic speaker, was elected among three candidates. That was the result after the organization's first democratic and transparent procedure, for which Turkey had pushed and of which several officials in Ankara spoke proudly. 'Another democratic achievement by Turkey,' was one of the comments made. As Professor Ihsanoğlu was preparing to leave for the OIC headquarters, based in the Saudi Arabian commercial hub of Jeddah, the mild-mannered and devout professor emphasized the need to increase understanding between different cultures and religions and to combat Islamophobia. As I said farewell to the future head of the OIC, he followed me out through the small but exquisite garden of his institute to my car and shook my hand. Thus far, I have never met any devout Turk who did not shake my hand and Professor Ihsanoğlu was no exception. When I met him at the OIC headquarters in Jeddah a few years later, in November 2007, he had not changed his views except in becoming much firmer in his commitment to prevent

Islamophobia. In the diplomatic corps, it is only Iranian colleagues who avoid shaking hands with females, but this is such a well-known fact that there are never any embarrassing moments when you end up with your hand being rejected and hanging in empty space. My husband always chose to play it safe when he met Turkish women he did not know by never reaching out his hand but waiting for the woman to do so.

Since the bridge-building EU–OIC conference in Istanbul, the picture in the Middle East and beyond has darkened considerably with rapidly deteriorating situations in Iraq, Afghanistan, Palestine and Lebanon. Ironically, the Middle Eastern democratization process has recently mostly benefited radical Islamist groups. The gains of the Iran-backed Hezbollah in the Lebanese Parliament, the Muslim Brotherhood in Egypt in 2004 and the sweeping victory of Hamas in the Palestinian elections in early 2005 illustrated the appeal of an alternative and untested Islamist approach. The root causes have to be recognized, which means real political, social and economic problems need to be dealt with, something that many of the OIC and EU leaders highlighted at the pioneering Istanbul conference on 'Civilization and Harmony: A Political Dimension.'

Meanwhile, the phrase 'war on terror', which was widely used in the US and Britain, as well as in Turkey, during the years following 2001, appeared to have been dropped by British officials in late 2006 in an attempt to avoid stirring up further resentment in Muslim communities at home and abroad. The military terminology was increasingly viewed by many, including terrorist experts, as counter-productive and merely contributing to increasing divisions and isolating communities.

The role of religion

Morning was breaking. The *muezzin* in the minaret at the mosque next to our home was calling to prayer. Only our sprawling, beautiful garden, which my daughter found exactly like that in *The Secret*

Garden, her favourite tale, was between our house and the mosque. The call to prayer was no longer made live but was a recorded message broadcast through a loudspeaker, which woke us up every morning for four years since it was very close to our bedrooms. During our first few weeks living in Ankara it startled my ten-year-old daughter every time but we both soon got used to it and found it comforting. It meant that we had another hour and a half's sleep before it was time to rush off to catch the school bus and get to the embassy. Strictly secular Turkish friends insisted the volume kept increasing in our affluent neighbourhood after the pro-Islamic government was elected into office. I knew that was not the case, being something of a local expert living so near the minaret. I soon found that the prayers, five times a day, every day, framed my day in a pleasant and structured way, as well as reminding me that it was lunchtime at around one o'clock. Although, while in Ankara, I did miss hearing the familiar, recorded voice of the *muezzin* mixed with the sound of church bells the way one could in Beirut. For that we had to go to Istanbul.

Rumours about increasingly intrusive prayer calls in my area reflected the mistrust between the staunchly secular forces and the new political establishment. Another such unfounded rumour was that the national carrier, Turkish Airlines, headed by an appointee of the pro-Islamic party government, was consciously getting rid of air-hostesses, preferring male crew. This had resulted in a lack of crew, causing constant delays for the airline, which had previously been known for its punctuality. The reality was quite otherwise. The shortage of cabin crew was due to a mushrooming of other Turkish airlines, which offered higher salaries and were thereby able to recruit many crew from Turkish Airlines.

The definition of religion is a sensitive matter in Turkey. Political and military leaders are careful never to describe their country as a Muslim country but rather one with a predominantly Muslim population. If one fails to make that distinction as a foreign diplomat one is bound to be corrected. Thereby, the staunch secularism of the

Turkish republic is always emphasized and, by some Turks, viewed as the proper way of safeguarding it at all times.

It was interesting to note the number of times Turkish local officials did not hesitate to ask one of the Embassy's interns where she originally came from, since they found that 'she did not really look Swedish.' She was a brilliant university student, who had arrived as a twelve-year-old refugee in Sweden. When she answered 'Bosnia', many lit up and replied 'then you must be a Muslim,' which made her somewhat uncomfortable since she was unused to being asked about her religious affiliation. I was never asked about which branch of Christianity I belonged to. The issue was only raised occasionally in association with the question of whether the majority of Swedes have the same religion as the Germans. Germany is a country which many Turks are especially familiar with since it has more Turkish immigrants (three million) than any other European country. Sometimes when Turkish officials seemed overly pessimistic and gloomy about the possibility of Turkey ever becoming a member of what they sometimes described as the 'Christian Club', I reminded them that when Sweden and Finland joined the EU in 1995 (together with Austria, which is predominantly Catholic), there were frequent debates about how the EU, with its incoming Protestant members, might run the risk of becoming 'too Protestant', possibly undermining the hitherto dominant Roman Catholic mentality of the EU. But once these predominantly Protestant but secular Nordic states had become members, the issue completely disappeared from the radar screen.

No one anticipated the major crisis between the West and the Muslim world that was around the corner when controversial cartoons of the Prophet Muhammad were first published in Denmark's largest daily newspaper *Jyllands-Posten* in September 2005. During a visit to the Danish capital shortly after the publication, the Turkish Prime Minister Erdoğan warned of the potential controversies ahead, since the cartoons were regarded as not only deeply offensive (one of the cartoons depicted the Prophet with a bomb-like turban) but blasphemous in Islam. It looked like the controversy was dying down when it suddenly escalated at the beginning of 2006. A few Middle Eastern regimes manipulated the situation for political reasons, while most leaders in Muslim countries abstained from having their religion hijacked by fanatics. When newspapers in several Western European countries went ahead and reprinted the cartoons as a way of asserting the right to freedom of expression, it sparked furore and rage across the Muslim world. The result was the gravest cultural clash between the West and the Muslim world since 1989, when the Iranian leader Ayatollah Khomeini called on Muslims to kill the British author Salman Rushdie for blasphemy. The clash became a power struggle between defenders of the right to free speech and expression, who wondered 'why don't the Muslims take legal action instead of taking to the streets?', and those viewing it as blasphemy against Islam and nothing but sheer insult and provocation.

The wave of violent demonstrations across the Muslim world, protesting against the caricatures of the Prophet Muhammad, created unprecedented friction between Europe and the Muslim world and resulted in at least fifty casualties, in Nigeria, Afghanistan and Pakistan among other places. Demonstrations also took place in Turkey, but unlike in Iran, Lebanon and Syria, no embassies were stormed or burnt down, nor were there any casualties. But the Turkish authorities took no chances; two hundred policemen surrounded the Danish ambassador Christian Hoppe's ultra-modern residence, located in central Ankara between the presidential palace and the American ambassador's residence, during the height of the cartoon crisis. Meanwhile, the Organization of the Islamic Conference and the Arab League signalled that they would push to make blasphemy and the violation of religious symbols illegal by international standards.

Recep Tayyip Erdoğan called for respect and calm in an article in the international press together with his Spanish counterpart José Luis Rodriguez Zapatero.[1] These two prime ministers from Turkey

---

1. *International Herald Tribune*, 6 February 2006.

and Spain, which historically have both been crossroads between East and West, argued that although the publication of the caricatures may have been perfectly legal, it ought to be rejected from a moral and political standpoint. There must be maximum respect shown for the beliefs of both sides and an interest in understanding the other side's point of view to achieve peaceful coexistence, they underlined in their article. With tensions running high, an Italian Roman Catholic priest was murdered outside his church in the Turkish Black Sea town of Trabzon. Until then, deadly attacks on the few Christian clergy living in Turkey had been almost unheard of. A few weeks later, the EU foreign ministers expressed regret at the publication of the cartoons in a joint statement after a meeting in late February 2006.

Since the bomb attacks in London in July 2005, perpetrated by British-born Muslims in the name of their religion, there has been increasing focus on the need for immigrants to subscribe to the values of the new home country. A similar debate on the need for multiculturalism to be a two-way street arose in the Netherlands after the murder of the film-maker Theo van Gogh. Tony Blair, a leading advocate of Turkish EU membership was increasingly alone after the political exits of Schröder and Berlusconi, expressed it by saying that multiculturalism was never supposed to be a celebration of division but diversity. 'The right to be in a multicultural society was always, always implicitly balanced by a duty to integrate.'[1]

Islam appeared in Europe during the eighth century, almost one hundred years after the death of the Prophet Muhammad in the year 632. An Islamic Caliphate was established in southern Spain for almost five hundred years, only ending with the fall of Granada in 1492. The Muslim threat against Western Europe was strongly felt during the Ottomans' long siege of Vienna, which ended in 1683, when there was a failed attempt to capture the Austrian capital. Surprisingly, I often heard Turks make reference to these historical facts, expressing apprehension that Turkey's Ottoman past would be

---

1. Speech, 8 December 2006.

viewed as a liability in the EU process and not only by Austria, where there is widespread scepticism towards Turkish EU membership.

Since the Middle Ages Islam has been established in the Balkans and until modern times European Islam – in which Turkey is not included – has mainly been represented by Muslims from former Yugoslavia and Albania. From the 1950s onwards many immigrants and refugees from Muslim countries arrived in Europe, the US and Australia. Today, Islam is one of the fastest growing religions in Europe and the US. It is the second largest in several Western European countries, among them Germany, the Netherlands and Sweden. Today, an estimated 20 million Muslims live in Europe, Turkey excluded. Interestingly, Turkey's population of 72 million is rarely included in any statistics on Muslims in Europe despite it being a fully-credited EU candidate country since 1999.

There are no official EU statistics on religious affiliation among its population of 500 million, but the number of Muslims is widely regarded to be around 20 million while some estimates vary up to 30 million. This makes the Islam of today a part of Europe and Europe a part of Islam. The lowest estimate is 13 million, or 3.5 per cent of the EU population, according to a report on 'Muslims in the European Union: Discrimination and Islamophobia' by the EU organ, the European Centre for Monitoring Racism and Xenophobia, published in December 2006. This was shortly before Bulgaria joined the EU, having proportionally the largest Muslim minority; around 10 per cent of its almost 8 million inhabitants. Cyprus has 165,000 Turkish Cypriots, and France and the Netherlands follow with between 5 and 8 per cent of Muslims among their populations. Germany has less than 3 per cent of Muslims among its 83 million inhabitants, of which the majority are from Turkey, as previously mentioned. But many of those described as Muslims here might well have a relaxed attitude to religion and regard themselves as secular. The total number of Muslims in the world is estimated to be more than 1.2 billion, of which the overwhelming majority (between 85 and 90 per cent) are Sunni

Muslims, which is also by far the largest religious group in Turkey. The mosaic of Islam is vast, just like the diversity of most other religions.

We had spent our family summer holidays in a small village in Provence for many years, and once I became an ambassador to Turkey there was great interest among our friends there, all locals, in discussing Turkey and the EU, always with impressive knowledge. But I have found that not only in the south of France, but in many other places within the EU, there is a widespread and common lack of awareness of the diversity of Islam. Its history, various branches and sects and internal splits are rarely known. In Europe, Turks with their modern history of staunch secularism are surprisingly often conceptually grouped together with any other Muslim immigrant, regardless of country of origin, culture or class.

The official trip of Pope Benedict XVI to Turkey in November 2006 was preceded by a frenzy of speculation and worldwide attention. It was not the first papal visit to Turkey in history but the third; Paul VI had visited in 1967 and John Paul II in 1979. However, it was Pope Benedict's first official trip to a Muslim country. Initially it was intended to improve relations between the Roman Catholic Church and the world's Orthodox Christians, whose spiritual head is the Istanbul-based Ecumenical Patriarch Bartholomew, as well as showing solidarity with the small Christian communities in Turkey. It quickly became much more when the spotlight was turned onto the sensitive relationship between Christianity and Islam, which was deeply bruised after the cartoon controversy only half a year earlier.

A controversial lecture by the Pope at the university in Regensburg, Germany, in September 2006, where he used to teach, sparked a furore across the Muslim world when he quoted a medieval Byzantine emperor, who linked the Prophet Muhammad with violence. Unusually, the speech had been written by the Pope himself rather than by his advisers, according to inside sources at the Vatican. Worldwide condemnation followed but the Pope's choice to merely regret and not apologize for his reference fuelled Muslim anger further. But his stand was also defended in some quarters. The prominent Lebanese law professor and former presidential candidate Chibli Mallat, a close friend of mine from my time in Beirut, warned that the threshold for freedom of expression had become too low and needed to be raised again. He pointed to another tragic dimension at play here, concerning the fate of Christians in the Middle East. They were increasingly threatened by religious intolerance supported by extremists in Muslim and Jewish quarters, a situation which needed to be remedied.

The Pope's quote was inappropriate, found Professor Mallat, but demanding an apology was unnecessary: 'Freedom is never having to say sorry.' Critics should settle for debating and disagreeing, not demanding an apology, argued the human rights advocate.[1]

The seventy-six-year-old Pope had previously expressed doubts concerning Turkey's suitability as a future EU member. As a Cardinal, before succeeding Pope John Paul II, he had openly opposed Turkish EU membership. As a successor to the Ottoman Empire, Turkey had always stood in permanent contrast to Europe, he believed. The Pope's questioning as to whether Europe could culturally integrate a huge Muslim community like Turkey into the EU added to the controversy surrounding his visit. Widespread anger and thousands of demonstrators fuelled fears of assassination attempts, frequently mentioned in Turkish debate. Top officials gave assurances, though, that there would be even tighter security than during President George W. Bush's visit. Meanwhile, a fierce domestic debate prevailed. The secular forces welcomed the Pope's visit, viewing it as an opportunity to demonstrate Turkey's secular and Western credentials. Some ultra-nationalists and Islamist circles, on the other hand, condemned and dismissed the upcoming papal visit as a crusade and an atrocity not only for Turkey but for all Muslims.

Unexpectedly, Benedict XVI's most challenging and controversial foreign trip in his twenty-month reign turned into a success. The Pope's gestures of goodwill, from making general but positive comments

---

1.   *Daily Star*, 20 September 2006.

on Turkey's EU ambitions to making an initially unplanned visit to the famed Blue Mosque in Istanbul, where he prayed, were viewed in Turkey as a sign of respect, even creating a new understanding between the two faiths. A vivid account of the papal visit and its symbolic impact was given to me by a Turkish writer, who describes herself as distinctly secular. She was moved to tears while recalling the Pope's gestures of conciliation.

The Pope's visit took on bridge-building significance that few had anticipated in the West or, in particular, in Turkey. After all the initial trepidation and controversy, Turkey could take pride in reasserting its history as a meeting place of different religions and cultures. It became a blend of religious and intercultural dialogues between East and West with strong political undertones.

Various ambitious political initiatives launched by the US, the EU, the UN and regional organizations such as the Council of Europe are all indicators of the newly arisen awareness of the need for a dialogue with the Muslim world, something which has benefited Turkey, especially during the years directly following the 2001 al-Qa'ida terror attacks. Rarely were meetings held in Ankara between Turkish cabinet ministers when this important aspect was not brought up as a strong argument.

Preventing conflicts within and outside our societies is a key component of the EU's political agenda. The dialogue with the Muslim world is part of that strategy, with the Barcelona Process being the prime instrument, in which Turkey is one of the member states from the wider Mediterranean region.

Among the EU member states, the UK is one of the most active in its dialogue with Muslim communities at home and abroad. Fighting terrorism is the driving force; by focusing on strengthening moderate forces within Islam the UK is thereby trying to stop the radicalization of parts of Britain's Muslim community. To quote Tony Blair: 'This is not a clash between civilizations. It is a clash about civilization.' In Germany, where the largest immigrant group originates from Turkey, a project was launched shortly after the 2001 attacks for a 'European–Islamic cultural dialogue'. It included German language courses for Turkish imams. In 2006, a joint Turkish–German plan was launched by foreign ministers Abdullah Gül and Frank Walter Steinmeier to boost intercultural dialogue. It was symbolically named after the German Social Democratic Party leader Ernest Reuter, who fled Nazi Germany and escaped to Turkey, where he became a university teacher.

When the EU decided to establish a foundation for a dialogue between cultures, within the framework of the Barcelona Process, competition was tough; several EU member states were keen to have it established on their own soil, while Sweden and Egypt proposed an 'Anna Lindh Foundation', named after the recently murdered young Swedish foreign minister, to be based in the historical Egyptian seaside city of Alexandria. Learning through my diplomatic contacts in Ankara that Turkey was supporting this proposal meant a great deal. It was of special significance to be supported by a country with such a unique role in intercultural dialogue and it went beyond my own sense of satisfaction as a Swedish ambassador, gratifying me personally, as I had been very fond of Anna Lindh.

At the UN, the Spanish–Turkish initiative 'Alliance between Civilizations' presented a report in 2006, filled with concrete examples of recommendations on how to avoid confrontation, ranging in topics from youth to media promotions. It thus moved towards more concrete actions rather than pursuing 'a dialogue about a dialogue', which was the tendency, at least initially, in many states and international organizations.

In another UN forum in New York, the Turkish government joined the UK in initiating the UN human rights resolution on work to eliminate crimes against girls and women committed in the name of 'honour'. The British and Turkish governments described their joint efforts to fight 'one of the most pernicious challenges faced by our societies' as a problem occurring in both their countries. The move, resulting in the adoption by the UN General Assembly in the beginning of 2005, was enthusiastically welcomed by women's rights organizations in Turkey, who felt they finally had their government's full backing in the international arena on an issue that in many countries had been conveniently pushed under the carpet for years. Turkey's position encouraged other countries in the Muslim world to face up to the problem, reflected one friend of mine, an academic from Istanbul who for ten years researched and wrote a PhD thesis on this problem in her own country. The UN action on 'honour' crimes reinforced Turkey's image as a bridge-builder, not merely in diplomatic circles in the UN Manhattan skyscraper but also among non-governmental organizations.

Abdullah Gül pursued a similarly important goal on the need for gender equality and other human rights reforms at OIC meetings, although I believe that this has never been properly known or acknowledged in EU capitals. Mr Gül, who was the outgoing chairman for the foreign ministers' OIC sessions in Yemen in summer 2005, stressed yet again the need for further reforms and an enhanced dialogue with the rest of the world. At the same session in the Yemeni capital Sana'a, the Turkish OIC Secretary General Ihsanoğlu demanded representation from a Muslim country among the seats of the UN Security Council.

Despite all efforts, the beginning of the new millennium brought an increase of obstacles to the further development and improvement of a dialogue between the West and the Muslim world. The unfolding conflict in Iraq, the detention camps in Guantanamo Bay and the lack of Western official top-level contacts with the democratically elected Hamas government in Palestine nourished a Muslim interpretation of the West as wanting to dominate the Muslim world and of having double standards. The long-standing, unresolved Israel–Palestine conflict has exacerbated these antagonisms. It must be not forgotten but prioritized and resolved, which would remove a crucial obstacle in relations between the West and the Muslim world, as Prime Minister Erdoğan and Foreign Minister Gül have repeatedly stated in their contact with the EU, the US and others. Unfortunately, their message seems to have been marginalized and overshadowed by daunting and complex events, such as the West's efforts to stabilize Iraq, contain Iran and find ways to combat Islam-based terrorism.

Since 2003, the bloodshed in Iraq has added to the widespread perception that Islam is under siege and victimized by the West. Meanwhile, the West's record in defending Muslims in different parts of the world, such as in Kosovo and Bosnia, and supporting Afghanistan when the Soviet Union invaded in 1979, is often ignored or overlooked; but these examples speak for themselves.

Europe can no longer be defined exclusively by Christian values or easy geography. But a barrier will always remain between Turkey and the EU as long as the question of freedom of speech is outstanding. 'I cannot even imagine the EU with a member that does not follow a principle so essential as freedom of speech. Turkey must, without delay, reform the law in question,' said the EU Enlargement Commissioner, Olli Rehn, in the summer of 2006, referring to Article 301 of the Penal Code. This article made the non-violent crime of denigrating the Turkish Republic, the Grand National Assembly or 'Turkishness' punishable, and resulted in headlines around the world, while creating growing doubts about Turkey's true commitment to the EU reform process. This effect was particularly noticeable among those already sceptical or hostile towards Turkey's Western credentials.

While the Israeli–Hezbollah war raged in August 2006, the EU Enlargement Commissioner struck a more positive note on Turkey, stressing its strategic significance. As a future member, it could become the EU's bridge with Islam, said the EU top official.

Turkey's efforts on the international scene through bilateral and multilateral politics to bridge East and West, including beachhead reforms and moderation in the Islamic world, have been overshadowed by the shifting success of the EU–Turkey process and its political and emotional ebbs and flows. Europe's recent loss of nerve over Turkey runs the risk of further widening the West's divide with Islam.

ELEVEN

Turkey's Future:
EU Success Story or Unfulfilled Promise?

'We build too many walls and not enough bridges.'

Isaac Newton (1642–1727)

When Turkey became an associate member of the EEC in September 1963, Prime Minister Harold Macmillan was residing in 10 Downing Street, President John F. Kennedy in the White House and Konrad Adenauer, Germany's first Chancellor after World War II, was still in power. The same year, French President Charles de Gaulle vetoed Britain's application to join the EEC.

More than forty years later, enthusiasm to become an EU member among the Turkish population has dropped sharply since the green light was given to start membership negotiations in 2004. At the end of 2006, 51 per cent supported membership, a third less than two years previously. A widespread sense of resignation, even discrimination, is spreading, as though whatever Turkey is achieving it will never be enough to pass through the EU's eye of the needle.

Turkey, given its complexity, is unusually difficult to predict and its history is littered with the names of those making the right forecasts at the wrong time. This time around, though, Turkey's bid for the EU is more convincing than before despite many remaining pitfalls of a domestic and international character, which will have to be taken into account for many years to come.

The difference is that there is strong commitment and a long-term view to achieve membership, held by the ruling AK Party. It is a government more self-confident than many of its predecessors. Despite having a bruised EU bid, Turkey is less fragile now. As long as there is a strong majority government in charge, pursuing a historic transformation, the chances of succeeding are greater than before. This in spite of the government's occasional air of resorting to ad hoc approaches, which negatively affects the process and deeply frustrates the EU.

Against most odds and predictions, the AK Party government has managed to stay in power during its five-year election mandate, being the first political party in Turkey to do so. Since the election in 2002, pressure peaked from time to time on Prime Minster Erdoğan to call for a re-election. His counter-argument simply boiled down to the statement that he had promised his voters to stay the whole five-year period and that's what would happen. The same strong-willed commitment to Turkey's EU bid can be found among his closest advisers, a fact often overlooked or dismissed in EU capitals. 'We have promised our voters to work for an EU membership and that's what we will do.' It sounded so simple and yet so convincing as the prime minister's adviser and I were talking in autumn 2006 with the shores of Istanbul as the backdrop. The same evening his warm-hearted wife, her head covered by a headscarf, unlike their vivacious daughter's, almost convinced me to have an eye operation to correct my sight, a rapidly growing business in Istanbul, as is plastic surgery.

The EU process carries on, although it is increasingly difficult for the government to motivate and justify reforms as part of the troubled EU bid. Turkey's refusal to open its ports to Cyprus resulted in the EU's suspension of eight out of thirty-five policy areas in the membership talks. In spite of this partial suspension of the negotiations in December 2006, Turkey has vowed to mount a 'do-it-yourself legislative offensive.' The Turkish ambassador to the EU, Volkan Bozkir, publicly emphasized this intention to speed up reforms so that Turkey can join the EU when the political climate has changed. The Brussels-based Bozkir, who was head of the political department in the Foreign Ministry during my time in Ankara, has the rare ability to create a 'feel-good atmosphere' even during the most difficult discussions, a much-needed skill in such a challenging posting.

The arguments for and against a Turkish EU membership will be frequently ventilated up until the year 2014, when it is assumed that the crucial decision will be made as to whether Turkey will join. It coincides with the EU's next budget period. No one, not even the most solid supporters of Turkey's eventual admission, expects it to be anything but a long and complicated process.

While Turkey's cultural credentials are increasingly questioned in key EU member states such as Germany and France, a quote by one of the EU's founding fathers, Jean Monnet, comes to mind. He said: 'We are not combining nations, we are bringing together people.' No Christian criterion exists for members to join. Almost twenty million Muslims live within the EU today, making Islam already an integrated part of Europe. Accepting Turkey as a full member – but only once the criteria have been fulfilled – would be a symbolic act signifying that the EU, which essentially started as a peace project after World War II, is able and willing to develop in new directions. It would also refute the perception among many Muslims in Europe of being second-class citizens. The emotional impact of a large Muslim-populated country like Turkey joining as an EU member could reduce the marginalization and radicalization among Muslim communities in Western Europe. Although the argument that a 'no' to Turkey's EU membership aspirations would result in damaged relations between the EU and the Arab world appears rather exaggerated, nevertheless, with bridge-building between the West and the Muslim world turning into one of the biggest challenges of the twenty-first century, the EU's relations with Turkey are crucial. It is a constant test of the EU's pluralism.

To perceive Turkey as a firewall against the crises and violence in the Middle East is wishful thinking. Instead Turkey would strengthen Europe along one of its vulnerable outer borders. In addition, it would enhance the EU's role in the Black Sea and the eastern parts of the Mediterranean, both of key strategic interest to the European Union, which in Turkey would gain a partner with increasing clout and credentials in international affairs.

It was often mentioned in meetings between the EU and Turkish officials in Ankara that as a candidate country, Turkey was facing an adaptation process, not a negotiation. Rules and regulations were set and constantly evolving and could not be changed for an aspiring member. It cuts both ways though. The generally recognized principle of Roman law *pacta sunt servanda* (agreements are to be honoured) is a part of European cultural heritage, something which the EU should respect and protect. Assuming Turkey will succeed in meeting the necessary obligations, a rejection, including a 'privileged relationship' rather than a full membership, would be disastrous for the credibility of the EU.

A Turkish top official with qualms about the EU reform process and whether it would pay off and be rewarded by the EU in the end was advised by the charming, outgoing British ambassador, Sir David Logan, in late 2001. 'Just get on with it,' was his recommendation as we were having a farewell lunch for him in a restaurant in the outskirts of Ankara, overlooking a lake and the Anatolian plateau. The British ambassador recalled how his country had been rejected twice in its EEC/EU bid but pursued it and became a full member.

The EU ambassador to Turkey at the time, Hansjörg Kretschmer, echoed this message following the French and Dutch rejections of the EU Constitution in 2005. He recommended that Turkey should stay focused on the reforms and ignore the ructions in Europe. But the referendums illustrated the controversy surrounding institutional reforms while also reflecting growing hostility to further enlargements. After the fifth enlargement with the entry of Romania and Bulgaria in January 2007, this increasing enlargement fatigue might accelerate among EU member states. It would have serious implications for a large and relatively poor Turkey. Firm EU supporters of further enlargement, including Britain, Italy, Spain, Sweden and Denmark, insist that the door remains open to the approximately one hundred million people of Turkey and the western Balkans.

A vibrant market economy, priding itself on being the fastest growing economy among the Organization for Economic Cooperation and Development (OECD) countries in 2005, was globally only surpassed by China. In 2007, Turkey ranked as the 17th largest economy in the world. Foreign direct investments reached record levels during 2006 (20 billion US dollars). A notoriously high rate of inflation has been reduced to 9 per cent, the lowest in thirty years. Turkey managed to recover from devastating financial crises in 2001 thanks to the political stability linked to the successful EU process during the following four years. The membership talks were able to be launched in 2005 as a result of the sufficient fulfilment of the EU's political conditions. The economic criteria will gradually take centre stage in EU–Turkish negotiations. The processes of democracy and human rights will no longer overshadow economics, provided that the process stays on track and that the new legislations are properly implemented. If Turkey manages to sustain an annual economic growth above 5 per cent and to keep down the rate of inflation, it has the potential to become the next economic miracle, reducing fears within the EU of mass migration.

The 1,760-kilometre pipeline from Azerbaijan to the Turkish port of Ceyhan was completed in 2006 and will carry fifty million tons of Caspian oil to the world market every year. It enhances Turkey's aspiration to become a regional energy hub for oil and gas between

Europe on the one hand and Russia and the Middle East on the other. The constant questioning by some European politicians of Turkey's suitability to join the now twenty-seven member countries might diminish if the dynamism of the economy is kept up.

Large Turkish immigrant communities, like those in Germany and the Netherlands, have mainly a rural, traditional background from Anatolia, with poor education resulting in problems integrating in their new home countries. This contributes to solidifying negative stereotypes and sometimes outdated images of Turkey in Western Europe, despite its gradual and in some places rapid economic transformation.

Turkey has a young population with 60 per cent under the age of thirty, unlike the demographic profile of Western Europe, where countries like Germany, Denmark and Sweden have recently been forced to decide on a higher retirement age. The average age in Turkey is only twenty-nine. Should Turkey join as a member in 2014, it would become the second largest country after Germany while the population of the EU would only be increased by 12 per cent.

The success story of the EU–Turkish process since the turn of the millennium could, however, turn into the EU's biggest failure. Despite the re-entry in Parliament in 2007 of the Nationalist Action Party, MHP, the 2007 elections meant a roll back for ultra-nationalism. However, if the prospect of a fully-fledged EU membership keeps diminishing, there could over time be a rise of neo-nationalism in Turkey. A sense of betrayal by the EU would linger in Turkey. The EU, for its part, would suffer a strategic defeat for the West while Turkey would face several geo-strategic choices. Integration with the Turkic-speaking peoples of Central Asia, rapprochement with former arch-enemy Russia or strengthening of ties with the Muslim world, including its Arab neighbours, are some of Turkey's potential options.

Meanwhile, the rift between the staunchly secular and increasingly nationalist circles and the government has increased. While the staunchly secular circles are not anti-religious but mostly embrace their Muslim identity, they are protective of strict laws separating state and religion, which the controversy surrounding the presidential election starkly illustrated. As long as the military is widely viewed by the secular establishment as the institution expected to step in and help out if the politicians fail, there is a deficit in democracy. 'The military is like a protector, it will always look after us if need be,' one senior civil servant explained to me. The US ambassador to Turkey, Ross Wilson, commented on the fierce secular/religious debate in late 2006 by saying that 'There has always been a certain level of cacophony and noise in Turkish politics and media' while noting that 'nothing worries me with regard to Turkey's continuation as a strong, secure, stable and secular democracy.' Meanwhile, the AK Party government and its supporters are struggling to find acceptable ways of achieving a new equilibrium between the secular state and religion. Creating a space for those wanting to express their piety through, for example, their dress code at a university or as a state employee, remains an unresolved question.

The EU process faces several serious challenges. Obstacles to Turkey's path towards the European Union lie within Turkey as well as within the borders of the EU. Turkish pro-democracy forces need more international backing, otherwise they will increasingly look as though they are chasing an EU pipe-dream. At the same time, any Turkish foot-dragging on reforms has to come to an end. The EU runs the risk of becoming too inward-looking if a brake is put on the previously vigorously pursued enlargement policy. The agreement on the EU treaty, though, might reinvigorate the process of expansion. Turkey, on the other hand, could abandon its long-held historical journey towards the West if the EU's position on new members hardens and Cyprus, northern Iraq, the Kurdish question or other issues appear insurmountable. If Turkey is lost, it would be a failure of vision, in which everyone stands to lose.

TWELVE

The Beginning of a Post-Kemalist Era?

Seven is a lucky number in Islam, and on 7/7/2007 the number of Muslim marriages skyrocketed. In Istanbul a special wedding party was under way at Dolmabahçe Palace, on the European shores of the Bosporus. It was the first European-style palace in Istanbul when it was built in the mid-nineteenth century and served for decades as the main administrative centre of the Ottoman Empire. Tourists of today know it mostly as a museum and the place where Atatürk resided when he passed away after years of failing health. When a large, prominent Saudi Arabian family held a serene and beautiful wedding party in the palace garden on 7 July 2007 there were only a handful of non-Saudis among the hundreds of guests. Abdullah Gül and his wife, who have many friends from their years living in Jeddah, were among them, as were my husband and I.

Within a few months widely respected and hard-working Foreign Minister Abdullah Gül had become a highly controversial presidential candidate. Surrounded by tight security, he and his wife arrived at the wedding party by boat. It was unclear if their choice of transport was for security reasons or to avoid the notorious traffic jams of Istanbul. It was an old-fashioned and romantic way of entering the palace garden to join the celebrations. Mr and Mrs Gül were in remarkably good form considering the political crises which were unfolding during the spring and summer of 2007 when they were the centre of attention. Would Gül become the first Turkish president with roots in political Islam and Mrs Gül the first presidential wife to wear a Muslim headscarf? The outcome was a surprise to most, irrespective of political position.

Historical crossroads

Turkey was at a historical crossroads from spring 2007 onwards. The polarization between the staunchly secular establishment and the AK Party supporters became increasingly evident. Islam and secularism were increasingly portrayed in opposition to one another, as though they were different religions. The parliamentary election on 22 July and the presidential election the following month turned into a referendum on Turkey's future. Two main issues were to be determined: the shaping of democracy and the interpretation of secularism. The Muslim headscarf, which all of the wives of the top AK Party leadership wear, became the symbol of the power struggle between the strictly secular and the openly pro-religious forces. The place of the Muslim headscarf in society is one of the most divisive issues in Turkey. Previously, there has been a tendency for the state to dominate over religion. The AK Party, which embraces Turkey's Muslim and Ottoman heritage in an unprecedented way, was up against a Kemalist tradition of rigid restrictions on religious expression. This explains in part the fierce and bitter tug-of-war that started in April 2007.

After the election victory in late 2002, Erdoğan promised that the AK Party would differ from its predecessors by staying the course and governing until the end of the mandate period, i.e. until November 2007. Rumours about a new election flourished on and off during the following years but were categorically rejected by the prime minister. He had made up his mind to keep his commitment and thereby contributed to political stability. However, unexpected developments led to a deep political crisis and brought about an early election.

The new general election became a reality only three months before the end of the five-year mandate. The battle for the nation's highest post, the presidency, triggered the chain of events. The position, first occupied by Kemal Atatürk, is sometimes misleadingly described as largely ceremonial. In reality the president holds considerable power by having the right to veto and thereby delay legislation and appointments of top bureaucrats. He is also the Chairman of the National Security Council. Some presidents, like Süleyman Demirel, chose to keep a high profile on the international stage while others, President Sezer being the most recent example, had distinctly limited appetites for foreign affairs. Traditionally the presidency is viewed as the symbol of Turkey's secular state. With the AK Party occupying two of three key governing institutions – Parliament and the prime ministry – the presidency became even more crucial from a balance of power perspective. The other powerful institutions – the military, judiciary and bureaucracy – are traditionally viewed as part of the strict, secular Kemalist establishment. Speculations were intense and numerous. The core issue was whether Erdoğan would defy the massive opposition from the Turkish establishment and still choose to stand as candidate, which he had every democratic right to do.

'Say no to presidential ambitions, Mr Erdoğan', urged an editorial in the *Financial Times* in March 2007, which argued that the stability of the country would be undermined by a confrontation between Erdoğan and the secular elite. Around the same time, President Sezer, part of the strictly secular establishment, warned that secularism in Turkey had never before been under such threat.

Meanwhile, the AK Party pursued a strategy of complete silence about potential candidates, thereby avoiding the risk of deep divisions within the party. It obviously did not stop others from speculating about who might become the next president. Defence Minister Vecdi Gönül, whose wife does not wear a headscarf, and the government's only female cabinet minister, the young jurist Nimet Çubukçu, were among those frequently mentioned.

Among the AK Party grass roots there was concern that the party would suffer if Erdoğan were to leave the party leadership to become head of state. That was the case when the Motherland Party's leader, Prime Minister Özal, left when his party's deputies in Parliament elected him president in 1989. As early as summer 2005 I came across this concern among the grass roots, who regarded Erdoğan as an astute and undisputed leader. Prime Minister Erdoğan's only indication about the future president in spring 2007 was that the candidate would be an AK Party parliamentarian. He added ambiguously, 'It could be a surprising nomination.'

Pro-secular mass demonstrations were held in major cities across the country before the presidential election. In Ankara 350,000 people gathered in April, making it one of the largest rallies ever held in the capital. Numerous Turkish flags, pictures of Atatürk and banners paying tribute to secularism were waved by hundreds of thousands of demonstrators in Istanbul, Izmir and elsewhere. Anti-EU and anti-US slogans were dotted along the procession of demonstrators, remarkably many of whom were women and girls. At a cocktail party in a private villa overlooking the Bosporus in July, I politely asked one woman, who had demonstrated in Istanbul with her teenage granddaughter, if the demonstrations were genuinely spontaneous or if they had been orchestrated by certain organizations. She was offended by my insinuation. 'We are not stupid, it was all unprompted,' she replied. I met other women who were of a different opinion and who were angered that the demonstrations were being manipulated by political interests.

The nomination to the presidency was uncertain until the very end. One Turkish ambassador, who worked closely with Abdullah Gül in the Foreign Ministry during 2007, told me he was convinced Gül had determined to become the next prime minister once Erdoğan had moved up one step in the hierarchy to become president. 'Mr

Gül's eyes simply glazed over when we discussed issues taking place at the Ministry after the summer.' Just one day before the deadline, which was on 24 April 2007, the surprising candidature of Abdullah Gül was announced but only after tough negotiations between the AK Party troika leadership of Erdoğan, Gül and the religiously conservative Speaker of Parliament, Mr Arınç. The largest opposition party, the CHP, chose not to put forward a challenger. Gül was the sole candidate.

Initially, Gül's nomination was received positively, even among opinion-makers in Turkey. However, the opposition to the nomination was rapidly gaining force among the strict secular circles, fearful of the AK Party harbouring a hidden Islamist agenda. There were deep suspicions of Gül's past as a former member of an Islamic political movement. The CHP leader, veteran politician Deniz Baykal, had pursued a tough campaign for some time against the governing party but had been rather isolated in his attempts to create a sense of political crisis. This was no longer the case when the military, which has removed four elected governments over the years, stepped into the political arena, spearheading a campaign to prevent Gül from being elected. In many other circles, at home and abroad, Gül was respected for his accomplishments as foreign minister and as one of the key architects behind the restructuring of Turkey, which facilitated a launch of the long-awaited EU membership negotiations. As the country's top diplomat, his skills were tested during four turbulent years on various critical issues such as EU–Turkey and US–Turkey relations, the Iraq war and Cyprus. Gül's brief period as prime minister after the election victory in 2002, pending an end to Erdoğan's political ban, went smoothly, just like the uneventful transition of leadership between the two in March 2003. Rumours claiming that Gül would not voluntarily step down from the prime ministry turned out to be unfounded. The shift on the prime ministerial post in spring 2003 proceeded smoothly.

A comparison is sometimes made between the political tandems

Tony Blair–Gordon Brown and Recep Tayyip Erdoğan–Abdullah Gül, although the parallel appears flawed. Unlike the British comparison, Erdoğan and Gül cooperate without major tribulations and leaks from the inner circle of any controversies are rare. Erdoğan's decision to choose Gül as the party's presidential candidate in 2007 illustrated yet again the well-functioning political partnership. In the West, the nomination of Gül rather than Erdoğan came as somewhat of a surprise and was generally welcomed as a sensible compromise. Meanwhile, the atmosphere was changing in Turkey, where the opposition to the nomination was quickly gathering momentum.

Parliament failed to elect Gül as president after an unprecedented intervention by the Constitutional Court, which ruled that two thirds of the parliamentarians (i.e. 367 deputies) had to be physically present to validate the vote. Just before the court announced its decision, the military unexpectedly released a much-publicized message on its web page, implicitly warning of an intervention while expressing its discontent with the presidential process as well as the candidate.

The Constitutional Court's controversial ruling meant the introduction of a one-third blocking majority. Even though Gül received more votes than the three previous presidents Özal, Demirel and Sezer, it was simply not enough. Erdoğan condemned the actions of both the court and the opposition, which had requested the court to pass a judgment, stating that the ruling was 'a bullet fired at democracy'.

Erdoğan regained the political initiative in early May by proclaiming that a new election would be held on 22 July. The AK Party was prospering in the opinion polls, circling around 40 per cent support. The CHP on the other hand had declining support (around 18 per cent) but was hoping to form a coalition government after the general election with its former partner, the ultra nationalist party MHP, which was confidently heading for a political comeback, surfing on a wave of renewed nationalism.

The political climate was heating up at the same time that PKK terror actions increased in the mountains along the Turkish–Iraqi borders. The PKK seems to increase its activities when Turkey is at important political junctures. This was the case when the EU gave a green light to membership talks in 2004 and before the 2007 elections; both times coincided with more PKK terrorism. As the number of civilian and military casualties mounted, military demand to fight PKK groups in northern Iraq grew and was increasingly supported by public opinion. When a bomb exploded in Ankara, killing nine and injuring dozens in late May, the military shifted its top priority from protecting and promoting secularism to defeating terrorism, which was proclaimed as the biggest threat to the country. Without much contradiction the military argued that certain terror groups were hiding behind democracy and human rights in their struggle to destabilize the country. During the turbulence leading up to the parliamentary and presidential elections, the sure-footed military re-entered the political stage, almost routinely. Gone were the previous years of relatively low profile in the wake of recent EU reforms, which had led to some institutional limitations of the military's power.

It was a fear-based but surprisingly quiet election campaign in summer 2007. Like the previous general election, the AK Party had numerous volunteers. In Istanbul, 150,000 people, among them many women, were canvassing the neighbourhoods. The booming economy and continued growth were key questions while Turkey's EU membership was a non-issue. Among the main parties, only the AK was pro-EU, but with nationalism on the rise it put the ambitions for an EU membership on the back burner during the campaign. The tough rhetoric against a Turkish EU membership by the then newly-elected French president Sarkozy contributed towards a cooling down of the once thriving support for the EU among Turks. The CHP was pushing for membership providing it was without concessions on the nation state, secularism and Turkish pride. The MHP, which was part of the coalition government when Turkey became an official EU candidate country, found the EU process so disappointing that it no longer considered it necessary. The CHP and MHP, which historically have different ideologies, were now united in radical nationalism. The main opposition was largely divided but had similar messages for the voters; the government had sold out the economy to foreign investors, failed in its foreign policy and allowed religion to infiltrate the administration and education.

Support from the EU during the political stand-off between the government and the secular establishment, led by the military, was viewed as too feeble. 'When our democracy was under threat, Brussels and Washington trod too carefully,' one Turkish academician complained as we were having tea on one of the picturesque Princes' islands outside Istanbul. She was not familiar with the unambiguous comments by Carl Bildt, the Swedish foreign minister and vocal supporter of a future Turkish EU membership, who at a politically very sensitive moment stated in a press release that the Turkish military had no role in the election of a president in a European constitutional democracy. The heat was stifling throughout the pre-election period with higher temperatures than normal. Many people I met while travelling around the country that summer seemed more concerned about climate change and its consequences for Turkey than the upcoming election, which was frequently described as the most important in modern Turkey.

The governing party swept the national elections. Exceeding its own expectations it took almost 47 per cent of the votes, far higher than the combined votes of the two main secular opposition parties, the CHP and MHP, which took 20 and 14 per cent of the votes respectively. The turn-out was a record high: 84 per cent of the voters, which meant almost 36 million people went to the polls. It was an astonishing victory for the AK Party in every region, including the Kurdish areas. It was the only party that attracted voters across not only geographic regions but also across ethnic and social groups. In Diyarbakir, 41 per cent voted for the governing party, illustrating what many Kurds seem to believe: that Erdoğan is the key to a future solution to the Kurdish question in Turkey. Five parties and twenty-seven independent deputies, of whom the majority were pro-Kurdish, made up the new Parliament. The majority were newcomers and among AK Party parliamentarians fewer were religiously conservative. Some liberals and former social democrats were among the new AK Party legislators, reflecting a slight shift from the right towards the political centre. The securing of a renewed mandate for the governing party was attributed to the flourishing economy and political stability. Many commentators viewed its victory as a backlash against the opposition's build-up of anxiety and thought that the AK Party in the end benefited from the military warning and the presidential debacle. A Turkish friend, who has always voted for the CHP, had changed her mind this time around. 'I want a civilian government, that's why I am changing to the AK Party,' she said matter-of-factly as we walked on the beach in Bodrum, unaware of how utterly unused I was to having friends or acquaintances declaring their political preferences.

Expectations among women's rights NGOs were met when the number of women in Parliament doubled to 9 per cent, the highest level of female representation in Turkish history. Disappointingly, the new government consisted of only one female cabinet minister out of twenty-four. Overall, the higher number of political parties and wider representation gave increased legitimacy and pluralism to Parliament. When Koksal Toptan, an experienced politician with an unmistakably secular image, was elected Speaker of Parliament in August, it was a significant change from his conservatively religious predecessor and an olive branch from the AK Party to the opposition.

History was made on 28 August 2007, when Abdullah Gül received 339 votes in Parliament, far above the number required to become Turkey's eleventh president. The eighty-four-year-long secularist hold on presidential power was broken. As expected, the CHP abstained from voting. More surprisingly, the pro-Kurdish DTP also abstained from supporting Gül, disappointing many moderate Kurds and fuelling speculation that it was taking instructions from the jailed PKK leader Öcalan.

Four months after Abdullah Gül was first nominated to the post and failed to reach it, he was ushered into the highest office, surprising many who during the tussle for the presidency assumed an alternative compromise candidate would in the end surface. In a low-key ceremony in Parliament only a couple of hours after being elected, Gül was sworn in. The military and the biggest opposition party, the CHP, were conspicuously absent. So was Mrs Gül, whose headscarf had attracted so much attention and aroused strong emotions during the previous months. The atmosphere in Ankara was noticeably calm and the mass rallies of only a few months earlier already seemed distant.

In his acceptance speech, Gül praised the maturity of Turkey's democracy, while also emphasizing the need to trust it. Secularism was referred to as one of the Republic's core principles and a way to eliminate conflict in society. His speech stressed the need for continued reforms and modernization. Ensuring complete gender equality for women was described as a primary objective. A positive message was given on EU accession. 'We can make it happen,' said the newly-elected fifty-six-year-old president, but resolute reforms have to be carried out. He also promised his 'door will be open to all'.

Abdullah Gül was elected by lawmakers for a seven-year period but a referendum shortly thereafter, on 21 October 2007, brought a major political change. The next president will be directly elected by the people, and for a five-year renewable period. This could pave the way for Erdoğan's election as the next president in 2012 or 2014, depending on whether the interpretation of the amendments applies retroactively or not. A large majority (67 per cent of the voters) supported the constitutional amendments, which also meant that the mandate for parliamentarians was reduced to four years.

The referendum was overshadowed by a string of terror acts. Clashes between the Turkish army and the PKK resulted in more than forty casualties during a single month in autumn 2007. The separatist organization PKK does not constitute a military threat to Turkey but the recurring ambushes and attacks outraged Turks.

Parliament gave a swift authorization backing the right of incursions into Kurdish Iraq. The conflict with the PKK had, to some extent, the side effect of bringing the AK government and the army together. This was illustrated when Prime Minister Erdoğan, for the first time, was accompanied by top Turkish military representatives when he travelled to a summit in Washington in November 2007. The meeting with President George W. Bush was held against the backdrop of the US congressional foreign relations committee's recognition of the mass killings of Armenians by Ottoman Turks during the First World War as genocide, which infuriated the Turks. US–Turkey relations yet again came under immense strain.

The stakes were high in case of a full-scale military raid against the PKK in Iraq; such raids would seriously compromise the reconciliation process vis-à-vis the Kurdish minority in Turkey, the stability in northern Iraq and Turkey's relations with the EU as well as with the US. Furthermore, a Turkish invasion ran the risk of being militarily inconclusive, as the previous three large-scale strikes in northern Iraq in the mid-1990s and 2001 had been. Loud calls in Turkey for a Turkish military operation in Iraq were initially left unanswered after political negotiations yielded results. Prime Minister Erdoğan was praised for his successful diplomacy under immense pressure during those crucial weeks in autumn 2007. However, a string of Turkish attacks were launched against PKK bases inside Iraq in December, which was followed by widespread nationalistic fervour across Turkey, apart from some Kurdish areas near the Iraqi border where demonstrations against the attacks were held. Internationally, only limited reactions followed the Turkish military actions. The attacks coincided with the arrest of the newly elected leader, Mr Demirtas, of the pro-Kurdish 'Democratic Society Party' (DTP) for having avoided military service, which is compulsory for men in Turkey. The party allegedly has close links to the PKK, something which its young leader, who has served ten years in jail on charges of being a PKK member, has repeatedly denied.

Consequences of Turkey's political choices

A maturing and consolidated democracy emerged after the two 2007 elections. An overwhelming majority of Turkish voters opted for democracy over secularism. The democratic institutions were holding up against immense political and military pressure. However, the political crises during 2007 revealed a deeply polarized society. Remarkably, the economy escaped negative effects during the crises due to more solid and therefore more resistant structures, contrasting sharply with 2001, when the confrontation between the former president and prime minister had resulted in the deepest economic crises in more than fifty years.

The number of political parties in Parliament increased from two to five main ones, making Parliament more pluralistic and democratically legitimate, better reflecting the country's political diversity. The fact that several parties this time managed to pass the highest threshold (10 per cent) of European parliamentary systems resulted in increased proportionality. It brought a reduction of the AK Party's mandates by twenty-three seats in the new Parliament despite its substantial increase from around one third of the votes in 2002 to almost half five years later.

The 2007 presidential election underlined a reversal of the hierarchy of power, which started in 2002 with the AK Party gaining power. The traditional urban secular elite, which until then had been in power since the founding of the nation, lost another core institution with the presidency. However, they remain influential, in some instances still in control, in strongly secular power centres such as the military, the judiciary and the bureaucracy. When Prime Minister Erdoğan proceeded with the highly controversial presidential nomination of Gül, Erdoğan became the first Turkish political leader who challenged the military and who came out on top. The AK Party traditionally represents the conservative, middle class Anatolian heartland with openly religious values. Turkey might be at the very beginning of a new post-Kemalist era in which some of the long-standing Kemalist principles will be redefined or adjusted. When discussing this sensitive issue with one politician, he cautiously commented, 'maybe Turkey has entered a pre-post-Kemalist era'.

These fundamental changes of power have resulted in a deeply divided nation. President Gül has the potential of becoming a unifying force in a country undergoing far-reaching changes but only if he and his party manage to bridge the gap between the different worlds existing among the population. A special responsibility rests with the AK Party given that it now occupies and dominates the core democratic institutions.

The drafting of a new constitution will be a major test of the ambitions and commitments to reforming and modernizing Turkey. Two major issues need to be defined: the relationship between state and religion as well as between the state and the individual. The EU and many others expect to see an end to the harassment of intellectuals and journalists in Turkey, implying genuine progress on freedom of expression. Serious improvements are also needed in freedom of religion and minority rights. In addition, the Cyprus question, if left unresolved, threatens to unravel the Turkish EU bid. A major challenge for this strictly secular republic is that a vast proportion of Turkey's mainly Muslim population strongly identifies with Islam, a traditional religion that focuses on the family rather than the individual. But this also creates a unique blend. President Gül and the AK Party government face a historic challenge to demonstrate that Islam and democracy are compatible. Turkey has come a long way in proving that. Within the EU, however, Turkey's eligibility for full EU membership is increasingly questioned. In Turkey, an emotional backlash against the EU has significantly reduced the magic of membership although a strong reservoir of support seems to exist. The EU is facing a historic choice of how to deal with Turkey – the most liberal and well-developed democracy in the Muslim world of 1.2 billion people. The world is watching.

Bibliography

William Dalrymple, *From the Holy Mountain: A Journey in the Shadow of Byzantium,* HarperCollins, 1998.

David Fromkin, *A Peace To End All Peace: The Fall of the Ottoman Empire and the Creation of the Modern Middle East*, Avon Books, 1990.

Ingmar Karlsson, *Islam och Europa: Samlevnad eller konfrontation*, Wahlström and Widstrand, 1994.

Patrick Kinross, *Atatürk: The Rebirth of a Nation*, Orion, 1995.

Andrew Mango, *The Turks Today*, John Murray, 2004.

Shahrzad Mojab and Nahla Abdo (eds), *Violence in the Name of Honour: Theoretical and Political Challenges*, Istanbul: Bilgi University Press, 2004.

Lady Mary Wortley Montagu, *The Turkish Embassy Letters*, Virago, 1996.

Elisabeth Özdalga and Sune Persson (eds), *Civil Society, Democracy and the Muslim World*, Swedish Research Institute in Istanbul, 1997.

Andrew Wheatcroft, *The Ottomans: Dissolving Images*, Viking, 1993.

Erik J. Zürcher, *Turkey: A Modern History*, I.B. Tauris, 2001.

The Holy Qur'an: Translation and Commentaries, Istanbul: Islamic Publications for the Holy Qur'an Association, 2003.

Commission of the European Communities: Brussels, 8.1.2006, SEC (2006), 1390, Commission Staff Working Document, *Turkey 2006 Progress Report*, COM (2006), 649, final.

Commission of the European Communities: Brussels, 6.11.2007, SEC (2007), 1436, Commission Staff Working Document, *Turkey 2007 Progress Report*, COM (2007), 663, final.

Index